Martina Saric

Technical support in daily life of Type 2 elderly diabetics

AF138567

Martina Saric

Technical support in daily life of Type 2 elderly diabetics

Based On "DiaSport" Mobile Application

Formal Sciences Series

Impressum / Imprint

Bibliografische Information der Deutschen Nationalbibliothek: Die Deutsche Nationalbibliothek verzeichnet diese Publikation in der Deutschen Nationalbibliografie; detaillierte bibliografische Daten sind im Internet über http://dnb.d-nb.de abrufbar.
Alle in diesem Buch genannten Marken und Produktnamen unterliegen warenzeichen-, marken- oder patentrechtlichem Schutz bzw. sind Warenzeichen oder eingetragene Warenzeichen der jeweiligen Inhaber. Die Wiedergabe von Marken, Produktnamen, Gebrauchsnamen, Handelsnamen, Warenbezeichnungen u.s.w. in diesem Werk berechtigt auch ohne besondere Kennzeichnung nicht zu der Annahme, dass solche Namen im Sinne der Warenzeichen- und Markenschutzgesetzgebung als frei zu betrachten wären und daher von jedermann benutzt werden dürften.

Bibliographic information published by the Deutsche Nationalbibliothek: The Deutsche Nationalbibliothek lists this publication in the Deutsche Nationalbibliografie; detailed bibliographic data are available in the Internet at http://dnb.d-nb.de.
Any brand names and product names mentioned in this book are subject to trademark, brand or patent protection and are trademarks or registered trademarks of their respective holders. The use of brand names, product names, common names, trade names, product descriptions etc. even without a particular marking in this works is in no way to be construed to mean that such names may be regarded as unrestricted in respect of trademark and brand protection legislation and could thus be used by anyone.

Coverbild / Cover image: www.ingimage.com

Verlag / Publisher:
AV Akademikerverlag
ist ein Imprint der / is a trademark of
OmniScriptum GmbH & Co. KG
Heinrich-Böcking-Str. 6-8, 66121 Saarbrücken, Deutschland / Germany
Email: info@akademikerverlag.de

Herstellung: siehe letzte Seite /
Printed at: see last page
ISBN: 978-3-639-48713-8

Technical support in daily life of Type 2 elderly diabetics

CONTENTS

LIST OF TABLES

LIST OF FIGURES

CHAPTER 1 INTRODUCTION AND MOTIVATION

This chapter provides an insight into the research area of the thesis. The chapter starts with the motivation for the thesis followed by the brief description of the Diabetes Mellitus (or simply diabetes) and its types. The insight into the self-management concept, which is the key concept of this work, is provided as well. Finally, the goal of the research as well as its context and approaches are stated.

My interest in the research of technical support in the everyday life of Type II elderly diabetics based on mobile application comes directly from my family environment, where many members of my immediate family are victims of this disease. Ever since I was a little child, I was confronted with the consequences of the disease, because in 1993 the first member of my family diagnosed with Type II diabetes was my grandmother, followed by my mother and then uncle. As I can remember, the news about the diabetes discovery was terrible. Slow medical progress and poor self-knowledge about the disease and its correlation with daily activities and nutrition were factors that made the disease more powerful than it actually was. Observing my mother through all these years made me think that diabetes is a disease which is highly dangerous only if the person diagnosed is not personally involved in the health management. Since through my studies of information technology I have learned a lot about technology potentials, I wanted to merge my technical knowledge with the health management to facilitate not only the life of my dear people and other diabetics, but also to explore the power of technology in the process of self-management.

According to the World Health Organization (WHO), Diabetes Mellitus or simply diabetes is a "chronic disease which occurs when the pancreas does not produce enough insulin or when the body cannot effectively use the insulin it produces. Therefore, the level of the glucose in the blood is increased (hyperglycemia)" (WHO, 2012). There are three main types of diabetes:

+ Type I diabetes (an insulin-dependent diabetes) is characterized by a lack of insulin production,

+ Type II diabetes (non-insulin-dependent or adult-onset diabetes) is "caused due to body´s inability to effectively use the insulin and it often results from excess body weight and physical inactivity"

and

+ Gestational diabetes (first recognized during the pregnancy) (WHO, 2012).

Almost 50% of Type II diabetics are older people over 60 years of age. The most important factors that play role in the formation of glucose in the blood are; the age, lifestyle and physical activity (Morley, 1998). The fact that 347 million people worldwide have diabetes, says enough about the prevalence of this disease. In 2004, 3.4 million people died from diabetes. This fact indicates the seriousness of this disease. According to forecasts of experts, cases of deaths could increase by up to two-thirds between 2008 and 2030 (WHO, 2012). Austria has currently an estimated number of 500.000 diabetics (ÖDG, n.d.) and Germany 10 million according to Zeyfang et al., (2011).

In order to significantly reduce these numbers it is necessary to involve elderly diabetics in the process of maintaining a minimum level of glucose in the blood or even in the process of complete healing which is only possible with disciplined self-management associated with the lifestyle modification (Mamykina et al., 2006). Lifestyle modification involves combination of diet therapy (low-calorie, low-fat diet) and physical activity (Orzano & Scott, 2004), (Mamykina et al., 2006). Maintaining the lifestyle improvements can be challenging due to several factors that represent obstacles; availability and cost of healthy foods, lack of motivation to continue with lifestyle improvements due to the slowly noticeable results and social factors such as not being able to fit in with current lifestyle (Lin et al., 2006).

For the purposes of this work, I concentrate only on the physical activity of elderly diabetics as an aspect of lifestyle modification. Due to the large number of existing researches on diabetes, nutrition and mobile applications, exploring the physical activity and self-management of elderly diabetics supported by mobile application represented a major challenge, not only due to small exploration in this area, but also because it has to do with elderly people.

Many elderly have troubles finding the motivation to be more active. Reasons for this are varied, from the simplest laziness to the fact that they do not have the knowledge about the correlation between daily physical activity and their disease. A large body of literature argues that performing the successful physical activity requires the self-management (tracking perfomed physical activity) (Mamykina et al., 2007), (Corbin et al., 2000). In doing so, individuals could contribute to their health management by noticing changes in their health condition and attributing those changes to a particular activity performed and therefore makeing changes in their behavior (Mamykina et al., 2006). The understanding of correlation between physical activity and diabetes might be gained through the step-up process[1] illustrated below.

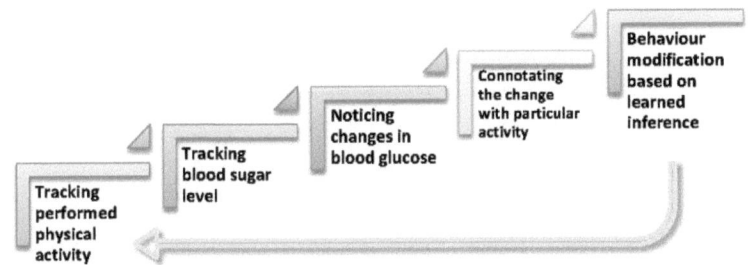

FIGURE 1 Understanding the correlation between physical activity and diabetes; the repeating step-up process; self illustration referring to Mamykina et al., (2006)

Another challenge with elderly diabetics is their knowledge about technology and their willingness to use it. Although there are many elderly who are already familiar with the latest technology, such as smartphones, there are others who are reluctant to use it. Therefore, the additional goal of this study was to explore how elderly would be willing to use the technology if they were shown the functionality and whether they would continue using it if they see the progress in their everyday life.

In order to explore potentials provided by technology in treatment of Type II diabetes I created a mobile application DiaSport (figure 2) that could test my assumption, that

---

[1] The diabetes and physical activity understanding process by Mamykina et al., (2006) is used only to demonstrate how diabetics can gain an understanding and improve their health condition through performing physical activity. This knowledge is crucial for motivation issues. In this work, I do not focus on improving the blood glucose since this research is not done from a medical perspective. Participants were not obligated to measure any medical tests to evaluate the medical impact as demonstrated in the figure 1.

such an application has a potential of being a diabetes self-management tool by encouraging the elderly individual to be more physically active. The main goal of applications such as DiaSport is to encourage diabetics in their physical activity by allowing them to monitor activities anytime and anywhere (Lin et al., 2006).

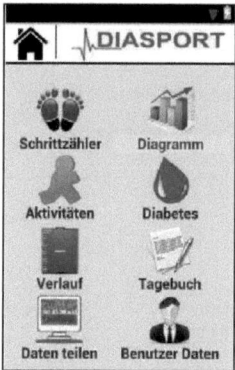

FIGURE 2 DIASPORT APPLICATION, HOME SCREEN

This research was divided into 6 phases; pre-phase (exploratory phase) (3-weeks), qualitative research (6 weeks), DiaSport implementation (8 weeks), DiaSport testing (2 weeks), DiaSport evaluation (1 week) and results analysis. Since I wanted to deepen my understanding about the correlation between physical activity and diabetes, I was exploring the lifestyle of diabetics that were involved in the pre-phase study. The aim was to explore how they perceive the disease, how they live with it and how they perceive the physical activity self-management concept.

The goal of the second research phase, qualitative research was; to find out how important is the physical activity in lives of research participants, what types of activities they perform and how. It was important to get an understanding of their needs and perception of physical activities self-management.

In the third part of the research, I provided participants with electronic devices through which they were able to use the DiaSport application for 2 weeks and thereby explore its self-management tool potential. The main goal of this phase was to explore the usability and potential efficiency of the application. For the evaluation of the perceived usefulness and potential effectiveness the participants were subjected to quantitative research, where they were given a survey to score the application performance. After the 5 phases of research study were completed the process of analyzing the data brought encouraging results.

According to results from this study, the biggest issue for participants is to find the motivation to be more active. Although some of them are quite active, most of them are still struggling with motivational issues. This is not such a scary fact since there are many young adults who are struggling with the same problem. Once they find the motivation (unfortunately, usually if they gain some extra weight or when their diabetes value is increased), they perform different activities ranging from simple housework to more demanding fitness exercises. An interesting fact is that every study participant is familiar with the importance of physical activity and the benefits it carries with it. The previously mentioned fear of elderly's poor knowledge about the technology and their potential unwillingness to use it is unwarranted, since almost all participants quickly learned and understood how the application works. Even those participants, who felt that they did not need such a motivator as DiaSport, were satisfied with the application since it was able to motivate them to be active and to make the activity be fun.

Yet the study has opened the door for the future work. Since this was a 2-week study I was not able to make any significant claims on lifestyle- and health- improvements. I was only able to test the potential need for such an application.

CHAPTER 2 THEORETICAL BACKGROUND

This chapter provides a theoretical background on the concepts relevant for this work. It will introduce evidences from prior researches that lifestyle modification through increased physical activity alleviates Type II diabetes followed by the move to increasing self-care management of diabetes. It also focuses on the potential of technology in the self-management concept. Finally, results from the research on existing diabetes self-management applications are brought forward.

2.1 FACILITATING TYPE II DIABETES WITH LIFESTYLE MODIFICATION-LITERATURE REVIEW

Type II diabetes is a disease that spreads globally at high speed. Besides the fact that it is a hereditary disease, the two non-genetic factors that contribute to the expansion of the disease are the lifestyle and obesity. Precisely these two factors have become a global problem, not only for the occurrence of diabetes, but also for the expansion of other diseases such as coronary heart disease, stroke, cancers, high total cholesterol, etc. (Tuomilehto et al., 2001), (CDC, 2011). Obesity is one of the biggest causes of chronic diseases. It is interesting that the problem of obesity is present not only in developed countries but also in countries where hunger is prevalent (Chopra et.al., 2002). Since it is not easy to measure the body fat, the most used measure to indicate the obesity is the body-mass-index (BMI)[2] (Antipatis and Gill, 2001). Chronic diseases associated with obesity are associated with a BMI greater then 25.

The main factors that cause obesity are; globalization of food markets, urbanization, economic growth and occupational structure based on less physically demanding work. According to Chopra et al., (2002), being obese in Brazil and Mexico is associated with

---

[2] Body mass index (BMI) is an index used to classify overweight and obesity. It is defined as a person's weight in kilograms divided by the square of his height in meters (kg/m2) (WHO, World Health Organization, 2012) (Vicki J. Antipatis and Tim P. Gill, 2001)

higher socioeconomic status and connotates poverty with itself. In such a world, where there are abundant unhealthy food and physical activity is just a matter of choice, people are becoming victims of diabetes.

Consequences of physical activity on diabetes are fat and hyperglycemia[3] reduction. It is therefore of great importance to seriously consider physical activity in everyday life and therefore reduce obesity. Many studies have shown the positive effect of physical activity on alleviation of Type II diabetes. In this work, since I am focusing on the technology aspects and the potential of the mobile application as a tool for the successful diabetes self-management, I am not concentrating on measuring of fat, hyperglycemia and diabetes values before and after the physical activity performance.[4]

According to Helmrich et al., (1991) physically active societies have lower rates of diabetics than less physically active societies. Physical activity accelerates fat loss and increases insulin sensitivity what leads to more successful alleviation of Type II diabetes (Helmrich et al., 1991). Helmrich et al. (1991) states that the age and body-mass index (BMI) are positively associated with development of Type II diabetes by males, meaning that, the older and the more obese the male, the greater the risk of Type II diabetes. Helmrich et al. (1991) has also shown the positive effect on reduction of Type II diabetes once the average man was practicing light-to-moderate excercises like jogging, walking, bicycling or swimming. Vigorous sport activities showed even better results, since they improve the action of insulin and glucose tolerance. The correlation between physical activity and the incidence of Type II diabetes according to Helmrich et al., (1991, p. 151) is shown below.

---

[3] raised blood sugar (WHO, World Health Organization, 2012)
[4] In order to see medical improvements, a longer study period is required (min. 3 months). For this research, I to goal was not to lean on diabetes values as indicators of effectiveness of the application (short testing period), therefore I wanted to explore whether this type of application is able to motivate people to be more active and the increased physical activity, according to experts, can lead to improved health condition.

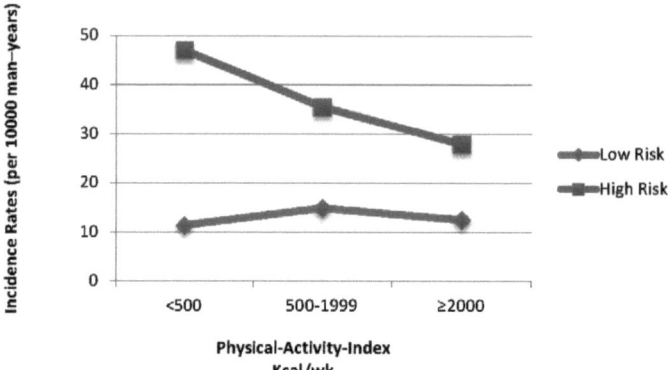

FIGURE 3 CORRELATION BETWEEN PHYSICAL ACTIVITY AND THE INCIDENCE OF TYPE 2 DIABETES (HELMRICH ET AL., 1991)

Men at higher risk level were those with body-mass-index greater then 25, meaning that, as they were more obese than those with BMI less than 25, they were exposed to greater risk of Type II diabetes. They also had a history of hypertension, a positive parental history of diabetes or combination of these factors (Helmrich et.al., 1991).

According to Hu et al. (2001), women who combined the maintainance of a body-mass index of 25 or lower and regualar exercise, had 90% lower incidence of Type II diabetes than women who did not combine these two factors. The findings suggested that in most cases, Type II diabetes could be prevented by regular exercise and modification of diet (Hu et al., 2001).

Another evidence of alleviating the Type II diabetes of both, women and men, with lifestyle modification is Tuomilehto et al. (2001). Based on this study, physical activities included both cardiorespiratory fitness and muscle strength. Results showed that people exercising more than four hours per week were successful in reducing the risk of the Type II diabetes. Exercising connotes not only vigorous exercises but also household work, gardening or similar (Tuomilehto et al., 2001). Recent studies have strengthened the importance of long-term physical activity due to the prevention of complications; glycemic control, prevention of cardiovascular disease, obesity, hyperlipidemia, hypertension and fibrinolysis (American Diabetes Association, 2003).

2.2 THE MOVE TO INCREASING SELF-CARE MANAGEMENT OF DIABETES

In cases of illness, from simplest colds to the most dangerous diseases patients are mainly passive recipients of medical care (Davies et al., 2007). Reason for such passive participation is an uneducated patient in that designated area of medicine. Physical activity of both, elderly and young people has been brought to a minimum due to the sedentary lifestyle (Zhu, 2008); spending lots of time in front of computers or television, chatting and creating virtual friendships and similar makes the physical activity quite impossible. Exactly this type of sedentary lifestyle is the basis for large number of chronic diseases including Type II diabetes. Self-management concept is a concept of teaching diabetics in becoming own managers of the disease. Modern medicine is forcing patients to actively participate in the treatment of Type II diabetes by modifying their lifestyle through increased physical activity. In today's world, where lots of things are done with the minimum requirements of physical activity, the biggest challenge is to motivate diabetics to start up and to do something good for the health. Educating diabetics about the disease itself and active participation in the everyday control of the own health status may contribute to the progress of treatment.

Since in many cases medical treatments are based on medications, most people want to contribute to their health by the active engagement with their disease. Management means that the elderly individual takes notes on every daily physical activity performed. Thus, the elderly individual can see how active he/she was in a particular day. An increased responsibility that diabetics get through an independent monitoring of daily physical activities and own condition afterwards can lead to more successful treatment of the disease. In many cases, people tend to lie to themselves that they have done something they have not or that they have done more than they actually did. Through the self-management, the person can track the history of activities and compare those with previous done in past days.

2.3 THE POTENTIAL OF TECHNOLOGY IN THE SELF-MANAGEMENT CONCEPT

As everything has two sides, so does the technology. Not only it promotes a negative impact on the physical activity such as sedentary way of life, but it also has great potential to promote physical activity (Zhu, 2008). With increasing globalization, we have come to a level where majority of adults own one or more of the electronic devices such as laptop, smart phone, personal computer (PC), tablet computer or even all of them. When computers first appeared, it was the perfect invention for which was thought to have no substitute. Soon after, laptops, smart phones and tablets have emerged and in some way replaced the PC. One of the advantages of the new substitutes is their convenience of carrying them anytime and anywhere. With changes in technology, needs of individuals are changing as well. Hence, the antique way of communication in both, private and business world is replaced by social media, emails and chat, the way we store and share information is changed as well as the way in which we plan and follow daily tasks. More and more elderly are also familiar with the latest technology either due to personal reasons, business duties or out of necessity. Although many elderly have difficulties with educating themselves about the latest technologies, using these might be very useful. This is especially the case with people suffering from Type II diabetes. Since Type II diabetes is the disease that requires active engagement of diabetics, modern technology can help affected individuals in managing the disease (Mamykina et al., 2008). Improvement and penetration of mobile phones for example, has resulted in the need and development of applications adequate for the health care management (Chomutare et al., 2011). These applications include monitoring of daily physical activities, diabetes values, daily intake of calories and other diverse data. Through building a history of such a behavior the individual is able to recall past actions and compare those with the current health situation. Therefore, the diabetic can make an educated decision with regards to physical activity and change the behavior if needed. The use of mobile devices in self-management of diabetes is not only necessary but motivating for diabetics. The fact that the self-management could lead to better health condition is sufficient to motivate a diabetic to make such a choice. In addition, there is an interesting side of the self-management concept; the daily challenge.

According to Klasnja et al., (2009), it is very important to encourage health-promoting lifestyle by making a support to individuals available when and where they make decisions that affect their health. Therefore, mobile phones may be particulary effective in delivering the encouragement since they are likely to be with the individual when they most need the support. They are also practical because they can be smoothly integrated into diabetic´s everyday life while encouraging physical activity. Achievement of positive impact requires careful design. According to Mamykina et al., (2008) it is from crucial importance to capture techniques with mechanism that can help not only to professional knowledge users but also to untrained individuals. Since the aim of technology is to facilitate the diabetes self-management, it is important to present it to the user as something that is motivating. Motivation may be encouraged through designing applications that allow not only recording of large volumes of diverse data but also engagement with the data, simplicity of data analysis and extraction of certain conclusions from the data (Mamykina et al., 2008).

Other issues that have to be considered when promoting technological encouragement of diabetes self-management are motivational factors. Motivating and encouraging physical activity can be a huge challenge, especially with elderly diabetics. It might be easy to encourage the individual to start the physical activity but the major challenge is to keep up the commitment and to pursue with physical activity in order to achieve the pre-defined goal (Byrne and Eslambolchilar, 2010). In order to motivate the user there are different motivators that can pursue the encouragement. According to Byrne and Eslambolchilar, (2010) enabling the user to share the progress with others and getting the feedback on it might be an effective motivator. Another interesting feature would be an aestethic reminder, like subtle wallpaper included in UbiFit (Consolvo et al., 2008) or in Fish´n´ Steps (Lin et al., 2006), both encouraging the physical activity in a fun way. Two mentioned systems were a motivation for designing the DiaSport application.

The following section presents various studies that investigated health management practices of individuals with diabetes and attested the potential of the technology in encouraging the physical activity and therefore contribution to the self-management of diabetes.

2.3.1 EXISTING INNOVATIVE APPROACHES TO ENCOURAGING PEOPLE TO BE MORE PHYSICALLY ACTIVE-THE POTENTIAL OF TECHNOLOGY

There are many physical activity systems available at the market, revealing information about physical activities performed. According to Zhu (2008), there are different technologies that contribute in diabetes self-management. Zhu (2008) highlights electronic devices such as mobile phones, PCs, tablet computers and pedometers. On the other side, there are technologies like accelerometer, Global Positioning System (GPS) and Geographic Information System (GIS) that might be used in each of these electronic devices and therefore contribute to physical activity self- management. Different technologies for the practice of the self-management are presented in the figure 4 below.

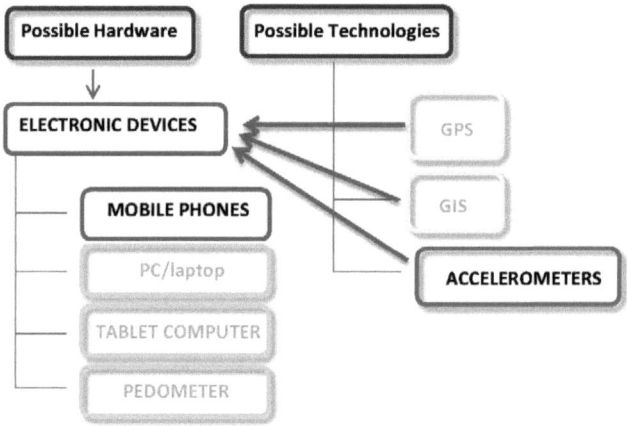

Figure 4 Possible technologies that have potential of promoting physical activity; red marking indicates technologies used for DiaSport application; own illustration referring to Zhu (2008)

Pedometer, according to Zhu (2008) is a portable electronic device known as step counter. It is used to record walking steps taken throughout the day. According to Bravata et al., (2007), the key factors increasing the motivation for physical activity are setting a step goal (10 000-step goal or an alternative personalized step goal) and the use of a step diary. According to this study, using pedometers decreases the BMI through increased physical activity and is therefore capable of improving the health condition. Accelerometer, according to Zhu (2008) is electronic device similar to pedometer, recording body acceleration minute-by-minute and reporting information on frequency, duration and intensity of movement. The major benefit of GPS and GIS is the tracking of where the specific physical activity happened which helps provide a better understanding of the interaction between physical activity and environment (Zhu, 2008).

According to Mamykina and Mynatt (2007) the significant transformations in attitudes towards healthcare are representing challenges for researchers, since patients are allowed to adopt proactive roles in caring for themselves. Therefore, new opportunities for computing applications´ designers are presented that assist individuals in the self-health-management. These applications are allowing the individual to be a decion-maker rather than passive subject of monitoring. Below mentioned applications that encourage the individual to physical activity are inspirations for this work. Special inspirations are Fish' n´ Steps and Ubifit Garden applications especially due to the interesting way of motivating and encouraging the individual to be active. In the following, I will bring forward seven applications that showed a great potential of technology on the self-management concept.

2.3.2 RELEVANT PRIOR RESEARCH

The **CHAP** (Continuous Health Awareness Program) application, developed as a traditional health monitoring application was developed to help older individuals with diabetes who spend most of the time at home, to manage their health (Mamykina 2009). Features of the application helped individuals track their daily activities and record their diabetes records. Since the data collected in the program were expected to be analyzed by the individual independetly of the eduactor, the application helped diabetics to learn new asspects of the diabetes management, but their knowledge was limited. Findings of the Mamykina´s (2009) study revealed the need for supporting social structures in order to produce reliable knowledge for the participants. Therefore, the second application **MAHI** (mobile access to health information), inspired by findings of CHAP took a broader approach including social components. The application was designed as a diabetes diary and experience sampling tool which allowed the user to interact with the diabetes educator in order to gain diabetes education and have an easier approach to collected data analysis (Mamykina 2009), (Mamykina et al., 2010).

Another example of integration between technology and health is the Aarhus et al. (2009) and its **eDiary** which is designed to assist the pregnant women with diabetes by allowing them to register their glucose values, record video consultations with the doctor and support video-telephone-consultations and therefore manage their health from home. An interesting application, that was an inspiration for my work is **Fish´n´Steps** social computer game and application, created to promote an increase in physical activity through connotating the player´s daily foot step count with growth of an animated virtual character, a fish in a fish tank (Lin et al., 2006). The game encourages both, cometition and cooperation with other players, thus encouraging the player to be more physically active. The game also includes calculations and feedback on burned calories, progress bar, personal and team ranking etc. The Fish´n´Steps application is showed in the figure 4 below.

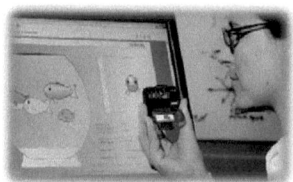

Figure 5 Fish´n´ Steps computer application displayed on the user´s pc (Siemens Global Website)

The purpose of the application was to encourage the motivation provided for participants in team condition where the winner was announced based on the states of the fish belonging to different members of the same group. The application showed to be very useful since participants were motivated to increase the level of activity in fun and engaging way.

UbiFit Garden, a healthy lifestyle technology uses on-body sensing, real-time statistical modeling and a personal mobile phone display to encourage physical activity (Consolvo et al., 2008). The application works like a personal journal where the user is able to enter, edit and delete daily activities performed. Aesthetic representation of the physical activity, displayed as the wallpaper of the phone, serves as a motivator of physical activity. The application showed fascinating results where participants were highly motivated by the garden figure that was increasing each time the physical activity was performed.

Figure 6 Ubifit Garden mobile application (Consolvo et al., 2008)

Houston is another mobile application designed to encourage the physical activity (Klasnja et al., 2009). It uses a pedometer to encourage users to increase their daily step count. The user is given the opportunity to keep a journal of his/her activities and to add comments on them, share experiences with friends and to receive a reward for reaching a daily goal. According to Klasnja et al., (2009), carefully designed mobile applications can be a powerful way of encouraging health behavior changes. This means that health applications must be designed with considerations given to how they fill into everyday life.

Move2Play is the application encouraging a healthier lifestyle through regular physical activity. It is made of four essential parts; activity recommendation, evaluation, motivation and tracking (Bielik et al., 2012). The main aim of the application is to encourage the user to be active, to promote a healthier lifestyle and finally to increase the quality of life. There is also a system for mobile phones that collects data from sensors such as accelerometer, GPS and GSM. In order to involve the user into the physical activity, the personalization is provided as well. According to Bielik et al., (2012) the most important part of every tool encouraging the physical activity is the motivation, since it is the reason why people start being active and persist in their activity for a long period of time.

Unlike above explored applications, DiaSport is different precisely because:

- It has an integrated step counter where the user can get an overview of stepcounts without entering them extra into the mobile device.
- All components are designed to fit bigger mobile phone displays and provide elderly diabetics with transparency.
- The application is not dependent on any additional hardwares but mobile phone.
- Algorithm used for the step counter is adjusted to the speed of activities performed by eldery people.
- Activities provided are related to elderly´s everyday life (walking with the minimal speed option).

Additional components and details on the DiaSport application are revealed in the chapter 5.

2.4 RESEARCH ON EXISTING ANDROID DIABETES SELF-MANAGEMENT APPLICATIONS ON THE ONLINE APPLICATION STORE

For the purposes of this work, motivated by Chomutare et al´s., (2011) study, I did the research related to mobile applications for Android phones[5]. My research included online research, Chomutare et al´s., (2011) study and online android market (Google play store). The goal was to find as many android applications as possible in order to test them and to explore what features do these applications offer and finally to conclude which features are most prevalent on the online android markets. The main criterions for choosing applications for testing were applications monitoring diabetes, applications with either English- or German-language user interface and applications presumed for diabetics rather than for medical professionals. My search was based on keywords "Type II diabetes", "smartphone diabetes", "application diabetes" and "glucose" indexed by Google Scholar and Google play store. I also researched Internet portals. According to my research, there are 35 Android mobile applications for diabates management. 22 out of 35 applications were offered for free and for the rest of them (N=13) I payed the price ranging from €1 to €2.99. I tested all of them in in order to find out which features they offered. Table 1 (Appendix) summarizes existing mobile applications for diabates management.

---

[5] DiaSport application uses Android phones as its platform

The results from the table 1(Appendix) reveal that 33 (94,28%) applications use tools for monitoring blood glucose. Physical activity and weight tracking tool were included in 12 (34,28%) and 16 (45,71%) applications, respectively. Only 5 (14,28%), 6 (17,14%) and 4 (11,42%) applications respectively had an education, alerts/reminder and social media integretion included. This leads to a conclusion that the development of diabetes applications is not influenced by social media or this influence is so far negligible (Chomutare et al., 2011). The most prevalent features, according to my research are presented in the figure 7.

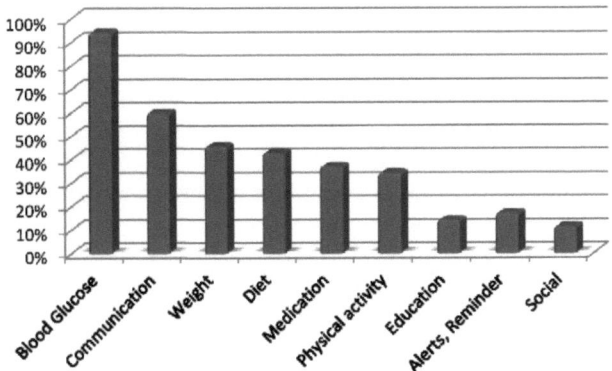

Figure 7 The most prevalent features for diabetes self-management applications (N = 35 applications) on the online android market

The major finding emerging from this study is that the combination of step count, physical activity and diabetes monitoring features is largely undeveloped. Although there are several applications using social engagement, I found that the concept is still seldom and that my application, DiaSport offers some innovative features. The detailed description of DiaSport application is presented in the Chapter 5.

CHAPTER 3 METHODOLOGY

This chapter provides a research description. It will state research questions and 6 phases done to exploring them. Each phase will be described in details. Since the DiaSport implementation phase was not considered as the part of this thesis, its *description won't be discussed.*

3.1 RESEARCH QUESTIONS

Following set of research questions emerged from my focus on the diabetes self-management for elderly people supported with a mobile application:

1. How do elderly diabetics perceive the disease and what is their understanding of correlation between the disease and the lifestyle (physical activity)?
2. What motivates elderly diabetics to be physically active?
3. How important is the social support in motivating elderly diabetics to be physically active?

    3.1 Are diabetics comfortable with sharing information regarding their activity level?

4. How elderly diabetics perceive the need for diabetes self-management?
5. How effective is the mobile application as the diabetes self-management tool that an elderly diabetic can smoothly integrate into his/her everyday life while effectively encouraging physical activity?

    5.1 Which way should be used to design constant reminder/feedback about activity goals?

    5.2 What is the best way to present an emotional state based on daily goals?

Following procedure occurred in addressing above stated research questions.

3.2 PROCEDURE

The study consisted of 6 phases as illustrated in the figure 9.

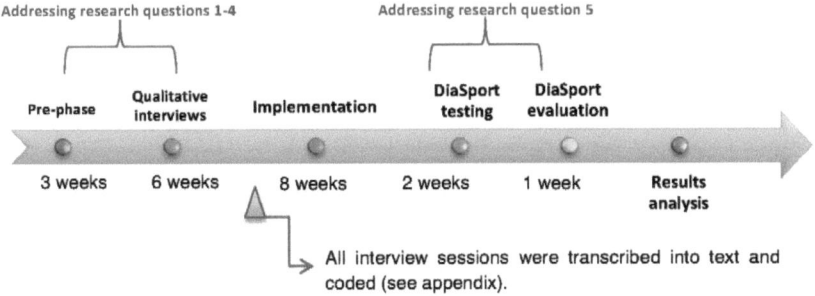

Figure 8 The research overview; the triangle represents the phase of transcribing the qualitative interviews into the text

3.3 PHASE 1: PRE-PHASE (EXPLORATORY RESEARCH)

Since at the beginning of the research I had a minimal knowledge about the lifestyle of diabetics, which originally referred to the lifestyle of my mother, a diabetic with whom I lived, I first wanted to broaden my knowledge. As I stated earlier, there are several diabetics in my family. I used the summer time I spent at home, to get closely acquainted with the lifestyle of a few diabetics. Deepening the knowledge entailed a lot of reading about the disease and treatment conditions, the daily involvement with diabetic patients and analysis of their relationship to disease and incorporation of physical activity into the daily routine. For the pre-phase I recruited four people; 2 woman and 2 men (aged from 54-60). The table summarizing the pre-phase participants is presented below.

	Participant 1	Participant 2	Participant 3	Participant 4
Age	54	58	57	56
Occupation	mechanical engineer	mechanical engineer	doctor	dentist
Diabetes history	5 years	10 years	3 years	6 years
Hobbies	TV and socializing with people	walking, TV, reading	travelling, PC, reading and playing with granddaughter	travelling, gardening and reading

Table 1 Summary of the pre-phase participants

I was able to daily observe the lifestyle of only one participant, my mother, while other 3 participants were only interviewed. All interviews were conducted in Croatian language. There were 35 open questions. In the case of incomplete answers I posed interrogative questions in order to get adequate and useful information. All questions were referring to the participants´ lifestyle, everyday life and their attitudes towards diabetes. Questions were also referring to their daily activities and how they get the motivation to be active.

The first participant, my mother is a 54 years old diabetic, with career education in mechanical engineering. She is married and has 2 children. Her hobbies, watching television and socializing with people, are requiring minimal physical activity. She has been diabetic for the last 5 years. At the beginning, when she was diagnosed with diabetes it was very hard for her to change her lifestyle. To gain some impression about her life as a diabetic, we talked a lot on that subject. I interviewed her asking questions about daily life, daily activities, medical advices and how these advices were useful to her. The interview lasted for 45 minutes and it was recorded. All questions were personal and interrogative. In order to explore the potential activity- motivator, I was posting pre-defined questions on motivation issues and potential motivators that could encourage her to be more physically active. The main goal of the interview was to enrich the knowledge about her understanding of self-health-management and her willingness to be her own health decision maker.

The second person recruited was my uncle, 58 years old and with the same career education as my mother. He is a married man, with 3 children. His hobbies are walking, TV and reading. He has been diabetic for the last 10 years. Unlike my mother, he is much more serious about diabetes and after being diagnosed with diabetes, he introduced strict nutrition rules and rigorous physical activities into his everyday life. I

TECHNICAL SUPPORT IN DAILY LIFE OF TYPE 2 ELDERLY DIABETICS | 2013

interviewed him at his house and the interview lasted approximately an hour. I did not have to post many interrogative questions, since his cooperation was more than pleasant. Other two pre-phase diabetic participants are one female doctor[6] and male dentist, both keeping their diabetes values to a minimum by the incorporated daily physical activity and healthy nutrition habits (eating small, low calorie meals five times daily). The female doctor is 57 years old lady, married and has 4 children. She has been diabetic for last 3 years. Her hobbies are reading, travelling, PC and playing with her grandchild. Our interview lasted longer than an hour, since she was giving extensive answers to almost each question. The male dentist is a 56 years old diabetic with diabetes history of 6 years. He is a married man and has 1 child. His hobbies are travelling, gardening and reading.

What I wanted to explore through an everyday observation and through interviewing participants is how essential is self-management for them in facilitating everyday life. I was equally interested in exploring what are their attitudes toward getting a feedback on both; calories ingested and physical activities performed. Since at that time the DiaSport application has not been implemented yet, I tried a different way of keeping a diary of diet and physical activities done by participants. I asked all four participants to weigh the food that they plan to eat that day and to write down the quantity in the pre-defined table. They were also asked to do the management with their daily exercises. They were supposed to write down the type of exercise, its duration and the frequency. At the end, before they submitted the diary to me, they were supposed to write how they felt after doing that. They were keeping a diary for 2 weeks. When diaries were submitted to me, on the basis of provided information on their height, weight and age, I calculated the number of daily calories they were allowed to consume. I did this over the already existing online calculators. I also consulted a fitness trainer that could provide highly professional feedback on their exercises done during those 2 weeks. After that, the participants were interviewed again. Two participants were tested individually while other two were tested together. As I daily observed actions of my mother, I knew exactly all the information about her attitudes towards physical activity. Therefore I interviewed her together with the female doctor. The reason for interviewing two participants together was just to find out how open participants are about their lifestyle when someone else is present. Since I had the data of other participants I was able to

---

[6] general practitioner

compare the data with the new data, which they provided during the interview. The only thing I could not be sure about is whether participants gave correct information about amount of food eaten and exercises done. Therefore I was not able to conclude whether a social desirability bias[7] occurred. The participants were given Merkur voucher of HRK[8] 50 for enrolling in the 14 days study. Due to the great distance from Austria, where further research was done, the 4 participants were not included in the further research.

3.4 PHASE 2: QUALITATIVE INTERVIEWS

For the qualitative research I recruited 10 participants, 6 women and 4 men (aged from 50 to 65, median age is 60). Participants were relatively heterogeneous group in terms of education and lifestyle. They also had different views on physical activity. While all of them had a certain amount of physical activity involved in their daily plan and program, lot of them was dealing with motivational issues. There were participants who performed physical activity rigorously and regularly, while others did not have as much desire to even talk about it. Even though some of participants were not motivated to perform any of physical activity, all of them were familiar with its importance in everyday life. A summary of 10 participants is presented in the table below, revealing information of their age, sex, occupation, hobbies and diabetes history.

---

[7] Tendency of person responding to questions in a way he or she believes is socially acceptable, rather than being completely accurate (wiseGEEK, 2013).
[8] The HRK (kuna) is Croatian currency

Ps	Age	Diabetes History	Sex	Occupation	Hobby
P1	55	6 years	male	technical staffing	fitness, walking with the dog and travel
P2	54	6 years	female	accountant	music, dance, hanging out with family
P3	64	7-8 years	male	retiree	gardening, chess, football
P4	53	9 years	female	marketing manager	skiing, travel, diving, running
P5	51	7 years	female	kindergarten educationist	sports, reading, bike riding
P6	58	4 years	male	professor	reading, travel
P7	65	10 years	female	retiree	tennis
P8	62	3 years	male	retiree	fishing, gardening, housework
P9	63	8 years	female	retiree	walking
P10	63	3 years	female	retiree	crochet, fitness, reading

Table 2 Summary of study participants (P)

10 participants who took part in the whole research were recruited through following paths:

General medical practices – I made flyers on which I briefly described the topic and the target group. In agreement with doctors I left flyers in their medical practices. Unfortunately, through this path none of participants responded.

Diabetes Associations – First, I found all diabetes associations in Vienna. I communicated their representatives via an e-mail where I described the topic and target group. Diabetes Association "Aktive Diabetiker"[9] was very supportive and allowed me to contact their coaches and to visit classes where they were meeting twice a week with diabetics. Out of 10 study participants, 3 were recruited from "Aktive Diabetiker" association.

Sport-Unions[10] - Since one of my friends is a sports scientist who works with diabetics 50 + and runs this program in a sport union, I used his acquaintance to get more information, technical support and to get to my target group. I recruited 5 respondents

---

[9] www.aktive-diabetiker.at
[10] www.sportunion.at

from the sport union. He also recommended "Sports Union Favoriten"[11], the association that is working with diabetics. Out of 10 participants of this study, 2 were recruited from "Sports Union Favoriten".

All three associations have expressed a desire to get more information about the study since they all thought that every diabetic should get familiar with self-management concept. Through sport unions and diabetes associations I made contact with the coaches. When I first visited their exercise hour, I briefly introduced the project and gave to every person a flayer with contact information in order to contact me if they were interested to participate. It was interesting that at all three places there was certain awkwardness present between them. None of respondents immediately agreed to participate in the study; they rather contacted me via phone later that day.

Most of them agreed to participate only under the condition of me helping them with the new technology. I realized that they were embarrassed to share with everyone how much they were familiar with the technology. Although most of them had a computer, some even used smartphones, more than 50% were interested only if the information they provide won´t be shared with others. Before I started the first phase of the study, I visited each group several times and trained with them, drank coffee with them or visited them at home in order to get closer to them and to create a more relaxed atmosphere. Through the hours of training we got closer to each other. Therefore, this research was really enriched with qualitative information. Most of them were already retired and had the desire and the need to talk with me. Many even called me afterwards to come to visit them again.

Out of 10 participants who were willing to actively participate in this research, 8 are born Austrians and two of them have been living in Austria for over 40 years. All of them had gotten the "geriatric" diabetes (diabetes in the elderly). 5 participants are already retired and 5 of them are still employed. 3 respondents have an university-education (pedagogue, professor of biology and an economist). The rest ranges from the medical profession to the gastronomy. Most of them perform physical activity only once or twice weekly. All of them have some extra hobbies, where most of them are passive like crochet or watching television. Socially they are all pretty active and always ready to buddy with others, but since most of them are retired and have no major commitments,

---

[11] www.sportunionfavoriten.at

hours spent in the society during the week are still minimal. After a lengthy relationship and meeting phase, participants were willing to participate in an in-depth interview. To motivate them, I gave each of them one REWE[12] voucher worth 10 euros. The interviews, based on an open-ended questionnaire, were conducted in German and lasting an average of 45 minutes. While questions were pre-set, the interviews were not strictly limited to the answers to these questions. Diabetics were asked questions relating their daily habits, their attitude towards diabetes, physical activities and importance of self-management concept and feedback that they would be able to see once preforming the self-management. Throughout the interview I wanted to explor how they perceive the idea of self-managing their disease. I wanted to find out whether keeping a diary of their physical activities and intake of calories throughout the day would increase their motivation to be more physically active and would that make their life easier. Another important research concern was to explore what are their attitudes towards sharing information with others.

3.5 TESTING DIASPORT

Application was tested by 10 participants described in the previous section. To be able to record the log data I insisted that everyone uses phones provided by me. Therefore, I created a test email for every participant, a Gmail, which they used during the testing period. All SIM cards used during the testing period were locked for in-coming and out-coming calls. In addition, everybody had gotten an A4 sheet with the text explaining features of the application. All phones are tested in the same period. Respondents were free to contact me at any time in order they had some difficulties with application. Before I gave them mobile phones I gave them instructions on how to use them. Each participant was supposed to fit the application in the everyday life and write down any additional features they thought would be from great benefit. In order to get reliable feedbacks, I told them that there is no pre-defined achievement from my side, and that any feedback is a good result for me, even if they did not like the way the application was functioning. Following data presented in the table 3 was recorded in the log data.

---

[12] a German supermarket chain

NEW DIABETES VALUE
NEW SPORT ENTRY
NEW STEP ENTRY
SHARE DATA ON FACEBOOK
SHARE DATA ON TWITTER
SHARE DATA PER EMAIL
SHARE DATA PER SMS
SENT DATA TO DOCTOR PER EMAIL
OPEN STEPCOUNT
OPEN ORDER OF EVENTS
OPEN DIAGRAM
OPEN DIARY
OPEN DIABETES
OPEN USER DATA
OPEN DATA SHARE
OPEN ACTIVITY
OPEN DIAGRAM DIABETES
OPEN DIAGRAM CALORY
OPEN DIAGRAM ACTIVITY BAR
OPEN DIAGRAM ACTIVITY PIR
STEPCOUNT STARTED
STEPCOUNT STOPPED
EDIT USER DATA
EDIT DIABETES GOAL

Table 3 Data recorded in the log data

My main hypothesis was that the DiaSport application has great potential of being a diabetes self-management tool and that it will have a positive effect on following two aspects:

🔸 **Motivation**: My expectation was that the DiaSport application will encourage the user to use the application more times per day and to be more physically active and conscious about the potential effectiveness and usefulness of the application in the diabetes self-management concept.

🔸 **Behavior**: My second expectation was that the DiaSport application will encourage the user to change the behavior if the application reminder shows low activity.

3.6 SURVEY-DIASPORT EVALUATION

The goal of the evaluation phase was to explore whether respondents used the application and if so, how they rated its functionality, design, efficiency and future usage intention. In order to find out, participants were given 15 statements, which they were asked to rate. All statements were related to their personal impression of the application. They were shown five-point Likert scales and were asked to give their opinion by choosing one of the five possible points. Finally, there were three open-ended questions included, where participants were given space to write what they liked the most about the application and what they would like to improve or change. They were also asked to write whatever they thought was important but not mentioned by me. To carry out this part of research, I went to each participant's home and asked them to be as honest as possible in providing their responses. Each survey lasted for approximately 20 minutes. The survey was conducted in German.

The survey template is presented in the appendix.

3.7 ANALYSIS

3.7.1 QUALITATIVE DATA

The qualitative findings were analyzed based on the Grounded Theory (Glaser, 2002). All interview sessions were transcribed into text (see appendix). Following Grounded Theory, the transcription of each interview session, with the relevant answers marked, was unitized so that each unit represented one idea expressed by the participant. Based on these units, a number of key concepts, relevant to the aim of this work, were identified. Each of these concepts was then labeled with categories. After this, the different facets or dimensions of these concepts were ordered into sub-categories and labeled as well. To speed this process, each category was coded, and the newly emerging sub-categories were added to the schema. Throughout this procedure open coding and axial coding were used (see appendix). Based on the emerging themes, a final list of categories and their sub-categories was established in order to get an overall structure reflecting the importance of each category. Using axial coding (see appendix), I was able to develop a short profile of each participant by connecting categories and sub-categories into a meaningful entity. Emerged themes from interviews are presented in the table below.

Diabetes discovery	Physical Activity (PA) context	Diabetes self-management (DSM)	Motivation
Diabetes phenomena (usual diabetes symptoms)	PA type	DSM importance	Potential motivator
Post-discovery emotions (first reaction diagnosis)	PA frequency		Visual records importance
	PA duration		
	PA/with whom?		
	PA social support/importance		
	PA information sharing/importance		
	PA achievement importance		

Table 4 Emerging themes from qualitative interviews

3.7.2 ANALYSIS OF DIASPORT TESTING PERIOD AND ANALYSIS OF QUANTITATIVE DATA

In order to analyze the results from the testing period I used Microsoft Excel as the analysis tool. I entered all the data saved from log data to the Excel file. The data (activities) that were saved in the log data is presented in the table 3 above. For each participant, I calculated the frequency of each activity per every day. For each individual I additionally added the sum of all activities performed during the testing period (2 weeks). That sum of activities per each individual is then merged into one table. Finally, graphs showing clear results were made.

For the analysis of the data collected from the survey, descriptive statistics was applied using frequencies in SPSS[13]. Following dependent variables were created:

- **DiaSport usability**
  - How often did you use the DiaSport application?
  - How often did you use the DiaSport Widget?
- **Perceived efficiency**
  - DiaSport application has motivated me to be more active.
  - This application has made my everyday life easier.
  - I found the self-management through the DiaSport application very useful.
  - I find the motivational figures really motivating.
  - I felt responsible for motivational figures.
  - Using the DiaSort in the long-run could help me stay fit.
- **Perceived functionality**
  - It is easy to use this application since the system displays the information clearly and understandable.
  - It is easy to learn all the functions.
  - Given instructions are plain and understandable.
  - The application reacts fast to all inputs.
- **Usage intention**
  - I will continue using the DiaSport application.
- **Perceived design**
  - I like the background pattern.
  - I like the application overall design.

The overall impression of the application was graded on the five point Likert scale and the data was analyzed by performing the frequency statistics. Final 3 open-ended questions were coded and categorized.

Final results are presented in the chapter 6.

---

[13] IBM SPSS Statistics is a software package used for statistical analysis

CHAPTER 4 FINDINGS FROM THE PRE- AND QUALITATIVE INTERVIEWS PHASE

This chapter brings forward the findings from the pre-phase followed by results from qualitative data analysis. Finally, it is brought forward how did these findings effect the DiaSport design decisions.

Pre-phase research has deepened my knowledge about diabetes and pointed forward some interesting requirements that were considered for the following research.

Diabetes knowledge

Interesting information revealed was, how uneducated were some participant about diabetes and its correlation with physical activity. This lack of education comes directly from the minimum engagement of the doctor with the patient and the disease. The first participant (my mother) was shocked with minimal instructions she got from her doctor after she was diagnosed with diabetes.

"I consider the physician´s instructions minimal. The only thing I got from the doctor was the diagnosis. After I found out I had diabetes I got the medication and I was told diet and exercise – literally 3 words. I have to search for the necessary information from other people with the same condition or through the internet."[14] Through her story, I realized that advices given by the doctor are predominantly related to prescribing the medication while maintaining minimum levels of sugar in the blood rather than motivating the patient to be physically more active and to change nutrition. Second study participant had the same experience pointing out the minimal knowledge he got from his doctor: "The doctor mentioned the diet and physical activity but he did not really point out the importance of those two factors. He gives a bigger role to medication then to sports. In time and through information acquired, I realized the importance of sports

---

[14] Participant 1 Gordana

even though I believe that the diet is the most important thing for diabetics".[15] Other two participants did not have similar problems with the understanding of the importance of physical activity for the therapy of Type II diabetes, since both were doctors.

Information sharing

Since the participants educated themselves about their disease through reading of books, online articles and other educated resources and also through conversations with other diabetics, I assumed that sharing information was from great importance for them. *"I learn the most diabetes-related information from other diabetics. Different opinions are always welcome. Since I know very little about nutrition and sports, I love to hear what other people think about it, what they eat, what sports they do and so on. Through conversation with others, I even got the motivation to daily walking, for one hour at least".*[16] The importance of information sharing emerged also from the conversation with other 2 participants:

"Talks with others are from great importance, not just talks related to the disease but about everything. We gain different diseases due to the stress, isn´t it then better to ease the stress by talking to others? We are not even aware of the fact that through the introversion and silence on every issue we cause surcharge, followed by the stress and therefore by different diseases". [17]

The participant 4 (Kristijan) was more skeptic about information sharing: *"I do not like to bother others with my health, instead they bother me (laughs). I like talking to others about sports but diabetes, not really".* This need to share information about everything can be closely associated with the personality of selected participants but also with the mentality of the nation they belong to. Croatians are normally people who like to hang out with friends and have close relationship not only with family members but also with a large circle of friends and acquaintances. Through this study I found out that, although the participants said they loved to share everything with each other, they had a dose of shame to show their diary results presented in the table 5 below. It seemed that they

---

[15] Participant 2 Zoran
[16] Participant 2 Zoran
[17] Participant 3 Edita

like to share general information about the disease but nothing that refers to their ambitions[18].

Diabetes self-management

All the participants argued that a certain kind of self-management is essential in order to facilitate the disease. The major issue is that they have not yet found the right way of how to manage the disease.

"It would be great to have something really small, like a watch that you can always wear with you. This should motivate me and warn me when I am about to make a mistake. I am sometimes really lazy, I need something to run me up. It can be some electronic device as well, but it should definitely be adjusted to an average person, without lot of *expert terms*". [19]

"It would be awesome to have a small electronic planner, where everything is personalized. I would love to receive everyday a good new recipe. That would make me happy (laughter). And I would definitely find new information regarding physical activities very useful. I spend a lot of time on housework. But that kind of exercise does not help me regulate my weight. I assume that a few tricks would help me achieve great results, I only need something to motivate me, a bell on the phone would be nice, but something else has to be attached, since I can easily turn *the bell down*". [20] I figured that they would all like to keep a record of their daily activities but under the condition they have the needed motivation to do so.

"I believe that nutrition is the most important factor and the physical activity is its best friend, the one without the other is not functioning. I keep diabetes at a minimum, and with a normal diet and daily physical activities I managed to bring myself to the level at which I was not able to be as a girl. I feel fantastic; I have a greater zest for life. I just regret I did not use to think this way before. It would be nice though to write everything down and recall it in the case I lose my motivation and gain some weight (or blood

---

[18] I found out that my mother was eating snacks and would not consider that as a meal, I thought she was cheating herself. That is why I argue that keeping a diary, not only of nutrition, but of physical activity as well, might be helpful.

[19] Participant 2 Zoran

[20] Participant 1 Gordana

glucose). But I am not sure if I have time to write every single thing I did during the day, *at least not now when I work".*[21]

Diabetes and physical activity diary

Since all participants were keeping a diary on their daily activities and nutrition I bring forward one example shown in the table 5 below.

Diabetes	7,2 mmol/l				
Meal	gram	calories	protein	fat	carbohydrate
pear	246	100.86	0.738	0	26,076
oatmeal	16	57.52	2	0,944	9,664
milk	200 ml	128	6,6	7	9,4
pasta dish	300	457	35	35	50
pear	324	132.84	0,972	0	34,344
lamb	26	19.36	5,2	1,196	0
bread	57	151.62	3,99	5,301	22,059
2 eggs	106	160,06	13,78	11,66	0
sandwich	160	287,04	10,72	13,92	31,52

11:00	**washing dishes**
11:30	vacuuming
18:00	30 – minutes' walk with my husband

"I feel great, I love walking. I even think we will increase the walking time, maybe an hour, I always have the feeling that I have more energy after this kind of physical activity". Even though I think I overdrove with fast food today, that sandwich was too much for my stomach".

Table 5 One participant's diary of nutrition and physical activity done per day, energy values are calculated by me based on an online calorie-calculator

Participants thought it was the nice idea to write everything down, because they were not able to cheat neither on physical activity done nor on some food eaten. If they cheated, they felt bad about it. Another interesting finding is that they felt this kind of diary was time consuming. Lots of calculating would present a huge issue for them. *"I do not have time to do all of this. If you can calculate this eveyrtime for me, I will be ok,*

---

[21] Participant 3 Edita

but to do it by myself, no thank you".[22] After the interviews on diaries were completed, I found out that two participants (participant 1 and 3) were providing more information in the diary, then in the interview. They probably felt they did not do as good as the other person and did not want to reveal details like in the diary. Two male participants were open about their activities and calories taken, since both were really disciplined even before this study.

Through the pre-phase I could conclude that one application like DiaSport could be of great benefit for diabetics. Since the market of applications relating to the measurement of calories and nutrition self-management is saturated, I decided that the DiaSport application will relate only to the relationship of physical activity and diabetes.

Qualitative data (full interviews with participants as well as their short profiles are presented in the Appendix) from Austrian participants has also enriched my knowledge and brought some interesting results.

Diabetes knowledge

Austrian participants had very much knowledge about the relationship between physical activity and their disease.

"Of course I am aware of the correlation between diabetes and physical activity. I do not perform physical activity only because I am a diabetic, but also because I want to be able to put my own socks on and to be flexible. That is the most important thing for me".
[23]

Only one participant (P10　) thought that physical activity has not much to do with her diabetes values: "I am familiar with the theory, but I have problems with the practice (laughter). I think that nutrition is the most important factor, I do not think that my blood *glucose can be reduced through performing an physical activity".*

Understanding of technology

Most participants said they would have no problems with using the smart phone technology, if somebody would give them appropriate instructions on how to use it.

---

[22] Participant 4 Kristijan
[23] Participant P7

Some of them use the smart phone technology and are therefore familiar with its potential in diabetes self-management.

Social support and information sharing

Since all interviews were recorded, I noticed that participants were stingy with words. They would tell me whispering, that they would tell me more when I turn off "that thing[24]" That led me to a premise that they do not like to share their personal information.

Most participants needed only social support from their doctor, their partner or immediate family. *"I do not need social support at all. Diabetes is my personal thing. I am not supported by anybody. My husband is not that flexible anymore and I cannot lean on him. Therefore, during the summer he is at our garden-house outside of Vienna and I stay here. I like the city. I play tennis or I go to the theater. He does not perform any sports but he does not tell me not to do any".*[25]

Another participant (P5) said: *„I do not need any social support, I do everything by myself and I am happy so".* Other participants, who are married, thought they only need social support from their partner. "The support from my wife is the most important. She knows what I love and what I am not allowed to eat. She respects it and cooks for me". [26] As most participants do not need social support, so they do not like to share information about diabetes. They only talk to other people about nice things and do not tend to discuss any private topics. "I do not like to talk to other people about myself and my private things. I talk to them about fun things. If I feel bad I keep it for myself. My *wife is the only person I share my private information with".* [27]

Some participants used to share information about diabetes with others but at the beginning, when the disease discovery was a huge topic. But with the time, they learned how to live with it and thought that information sharing is only bothering others. Most of them found sharing information as a suppression. It was interesting that only two non-Austrian respondents said they could imagine themselves in a social group in which they could exchange their personal information with other diabetics.   As I already mentioned in the pre-phase findings chapter, this has to do a lot with the nation

---

[24] That is how participants referred to the voice recorder
[25] Participant P7
[26] Participant P6
[27] Participant P6

mentality. According to Hofstede´s cultural dimension (Soares et al., 2007), Austria is an individualistic[28] country where people appreciate independence and self-reliance. They promote their own goals and desires, taking care of themselves including only members of immediate family. Therefore, information-share and wide social support for them is not of an great importance as for Croatians (collectivistic culture[29]). [30]

Performance of physical activities

Mostly, participants entertain themselves at home through housework, reading or similar. While there were many of them who liked to exercise and were sports "addicts", many of diabetics forced themselves to perform a physical activity. Even during the hours I spent with them training, they were more talking then exercising. Most of them have changed their lifestyles after they were diagnosed with Type II diabetes. This lifestyle modification mostly involved nutrition changes. While this was an easier task most of them had a problem with finding the motivation to exercise. *"I simply cannot find the long-term motivation to be active. I understand the consequences. I am also aware of the fact that being active would help me avoid medications but at the end of the day I rather sit in front of the TV and watch something rather than do something".* [31]

In most cases the main motivators of physical activity are bad diabetes values, gained weight and bad feelings. "I am physically active, but when I lose the motivation I find it if I see bad diabetes value and some extra kilos". [32] Once they find the motivation through either factors previously mentioned or through sunny days, they perform activities ranging from riding a bike, walking and gardening to fitness, tennis, swimming, skiing and dancing. All of the participants try to make some small changes in their lives such as climbing the stairs instead of using the elevator, going to work by bicycle or walking instead of using public transportation and similar. Even though some of them have motivation problems, it is clear that all of them have an understanding of correlation between physical activity and their well-being. Therefore, it is of great importance for all of them to find appropriate way of increasing their motivation to be more active.

---

[28] http://www.andrews.edu/~tidwell/bsad560/HofstedeIndividualism.html
[29] A collectivist culture is one in which people find needs of the group more important than individual needs and people view themselves as members of a group (family, friends etc.)
[30] Comparing cross-national data is not a focus of this work but this finding is an interesting remark.
[31] Participant P3
[32] Participant P1

Importance of self-management and potential physical activity motivator

All participants believe that a self-management concept (registration of the activities being done) is of great importance. While only one out of ten participants, P5, keeps a diary on her activities, others did not find the right way to do this because they believe that the classic writing in the note-book is quite stressful.

"It would be great to have something like a watch, that beeps to remind me to be active, to remind me when to eat, when to measure my diabetes and similar". [33]

„I'm the type of person who takes a lot of notes and records. But I haven´t found so far a suitable method to record my activities. I only take notes on my diabetes values but I think it is important for everyone to take notes in order to achieve some results". [34] One participant pointed out that the self-management must be fun in order for participant to be consistent in doing it.

"It is important to keep track of duration and intensity. There has to be difference between 30-minutes walking and 30-minutes running. Otherwise, it does not make any sense". [35] Participants think that any kind of self-management could contribute to both, the motivation and recall of past activities that could help change a certain behavior. Eight out of ten participants found a "figure motivator"[36] as an interesting motivator for self-management.

Since the qualitative data revealed information about participants´ life with diabetes I concluded that they do not like to stand out from others because of their disease. Even though they all had some post-discovery shocks, they learnt fast how to live with it. Therefore, it was important to consider following requirements for application design.

It was clear that the application should not be directly associated with diabetes, starting from its name. Although "Dia" indicates application for diabetics, "Sport" is a part of the name, which is a much more dominant and gives the impression of an application for sports rather then for diabetes. Since all participants measure regulary diabetes values and keep those saved in order to compare them with previous measures, I found it was

---

[33] Participant P3
[34] Participant P1
[35] Participant P4
[36] Figure like cat or flower that would change based on the level of activity and therefore represent a activity motivator

very important to enable the function of entering and saving diabetes values into the application and also making some notes on those. I also realized that for most participants simplicity is essential. Therefore, the simplier the application, the better. Simplicity refers to simple and easy usage and easy data overview and analysis. Since participants revealed they did not like to share their disease with others, I had to consider how to save the data provided through using the application. Although the results revealed that information sharing is not an interesting feature for participants, I felt that the data sharing option might be interesting because it could be used to share the data with the doctor. Since the data showed that participants engage in various activities, it was important to include a large number of different activities associated with the everyday life of older people. Due to the lack of motivation needed to performe activities, it was important to consider the best way to encourage motivation. To summarize it all, following requirements for application design were considered:

+ Name not directly associated with the disease
+ Possibility of entering the diabetes value and notes on those
+ Simplicity of data use and analysis
+ Data share
+ Locally stored data
+ Wide range of activities
+ Motivational promoter

CHAPTER 5 DIASPORT

This chapter provides detailed information on DiaSport application and its components. Inspired by the pre-and qualitative interviews-phase described in the previous chapter, DiaSport application was designed to meet individual needs.

5.1 DIASPORT DESIGN

Figure 9 DiaSport widget; flowers

DiaSport application is a mobile phone application that was created for elderly diabetics as a tool for diabetes self-management. Inspired by Lin et al., (2006), Consolvo et al., (2008), Mamykina (2009) and other applications for health management mentioned previously, DiaSport was created to encourage elderly diabetics in increasing daily physical activity. The application was developed for android phones as its main platform. DiaSport includes following components:

An integrated step counter- the user has an overview of steps count and can save the recorded count together with the calorie consumption. An overview of all steps counted and calories consumed per day are provided in the order of events. Additionally, total calories consumed are found in the diary as well.

Diagrams are displaying following values:

o Diabetes values: minimum, maximum, average, upper limit and lower limit per month

o Activities: 10 most performed activities per month

o Calorie consumption: through step counter, through activities performed and overall calorie consumption

o Activities in percentage (%): The frequency of performed activities displayed in percentage

Activities: The user can record an everyday activity and its duration. The overview can be found in the order of events component. Calories consumed during the particular activity can be found in the diary.

Diabetes: The user can enter new diabetes value and make some notes. The overview of all diabetes values recorded can be found in the order of events. The average diabetes value per day can be found in the diary.

Order of events: All physical activities performed per day, diabetes overview with displayed calories consumed and notes taken are found in the order of events. Each value can be deleted.

Diary: Diary contains information on average diabetes value before and after the meal, an estimated HbA1c[37], calorie consumption, step count and notes per day.

Data share: the possibility of sharing the data via sms, email, Twitter and Facebook.

---

[37] HbA1c occurs when red blood cells joins with glucose. The more glucose found in the blood the more glycated hemoglobin (HbA1c) will be present (Diabetes.co.uk the global diabetes community)

User data: the user can add, edit or delete following values:

- weight, height and age
- BMI and its intepretation
- Limitvalue for the low- or high blood sugar
- Motivational figure

Since accelerometers are inexpensive, reliable and practical, they are becoming a widely accepted and useful tool for capturing and analyzing physical activity (Khan, 2011). Since they have the capability of monitoring both, frequency and intensity of physical movements they are superior to pedometers, which are attenuated by impact or tilt (Khan, 2011). For DiaSport application, the first component implemented was an accelerometer-type step counter using a tri-axial accelerometer sensor which is integrated into every Android phone (figure 10). For creation of accelerometer-type step counter I used Horita et al´s., (2008) proposition of simple algorithm for the elderly who walked either very low speed or shuffled walk. The accuracy of the step counter was tested on 6 elderly people. Results revealed are presented in the table 6.

Figure 10 Accelerometer- type step counter implemented in DiaSport

Test person (age)	Counted number of steps	Number of steps calculated by the application	The position of the mobile phone
1 (62)	95	87	in hand
1 (62)	76	80	in jacket pocket
2 (65)	75	79	in jacket pocket
2 (65)	98	87	in jacket pocket
3 (54)	150	131	in hand
3 (54)	170	153	in jacket pocket
4 (58)	90	83	in jeans pocket
4 (58)	108	118	in jeans pocket
5 (52)	220	198	in jacket pocket
5 (52)	105	93	in jacket pocket
6 (63)	101	82	in hand
6 (63)	85	83	in jacket pocket

Table 6 Step counter accuracy results

According to the differences between actual steps made and number of steps calculated by DiaSport shown in the table 4, the small deviations from real step counts are not significant.

Due to the results from the qualitative data (fear of elderly people to share their data with others and high concern about privacy), DiaSport application was implemented so that all data is stored locally on the phone. There is no synchronization with either the server or some other applications. The only possibility of sharing the data is the one of following which user chooses voluntarily; sms, email, Facebook or Twitter. The user has the possibility of sharing the data with either friends or the doctor. At the beginning of the application installation, each user must give values on its height, weight, age and gender. The user is also obligated to give the email address in order to install the application.

Figure 11 DiaSport application; enter of values of height, weight, age, gender and e-mail

Since people do different activities during the day, it was very important for me to include as many distinct activities as possible into the activity recognition system. In addition to various sports activities, DiaSport also includes a list of activities favorite among elderly people and a lot of daily ongoing activities such as: aerobics, fishing, clean up, car wash, mountaineering, occupation activities (medium intensive standing activity), ironing, gardening, walking (slow 4km / h), cooking, playing with children (walk), Nordic walking (slowly, 4km / h), carpet or floor sweeping, climbing up the stairs, climbing down the stairs etc.

In addition to adding different physical activities, the user can also add its diabetes values with which he/she can easily choose keywords that are important for diabetics such as: before breakfast, after breakfast, before lunch, after lunch, before dinner, after dinner, before snack, after the snack, sober, before the physical activity, after physical activity, after intensive sports, before bedtime, at night.

All values of physical activities, diabetes and all notes entered can be seen in daily observations (order of events). Consumed calories per activity and steps count are also displayed. All measurements of calorie consumption are calculated individually by weight and gender of the user, and given metabolic equivalent of task (MET) values of different activities:

> Female: MET*0,9 kcal[38] * body weight (kg) = kcal/hour (ÖSTERREICH-GP, 2012)

> Male: MET* 1 kcal * body weight (kg) = kcal/hour (ÖSTERREICH-GP, 2012).

---

[38] Calory (kcal)

Average daily value of diabetes, before and after meals and glycated hemoglobin or glycosylated hemoglobin (HbA1c) can be seen in the diary. There are also total caloric values consumed per day as well as all notes that the user enters on the daily basis. Each user can choose which measurement units to use to measure diabetes. The user is free to change the height, weight and age. Based on given data, user´s BMI is displayed along with supporting information on the meaning of BMI value.

Each user has the possibility to define individual limit values for the minimum and maximum value of diabetes (either hypoglycemia or to high blood sugar levels). Through a diagram developed based on the daily data entry, the user is able to see a monthly overview, minimum, maximum and average diabetes values and the two limit values. Therefore, user always has a simple overview of his sugar fluctuations during the month. Diagram enables the user to see the calorie consumption during the month as well as the progress and development, and 10 most used activities. Each user can share own data via mail, sms, twitter and Facebook.

For all share possibilities, independent of each other, the user can choose what to share. Additionally there is the possibility of sending via email, all diabetes values of the last three months to the doctor.

The simplicity of the application allows a user to analyze the data independently from the diabetes educator and allows him/her to easily extract conclusions that emerge from the data.

5.2 DIASPORT APP WIDGET

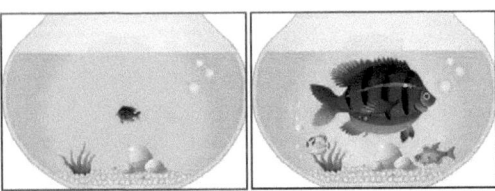

Figure 12 DiaSport widget; fish; inspired by Lin et al., (2006)

Figure 13 DiaSport widget; flowers; inspired by Consolvo et al., (2008)

As part of the application, I created the Widget that is inspired by Fish´n´Steps and UbiFit application (Lin et al., 2006), (Consolvo et al., 2008). Widget shows the figure which is chosen independently by the user. The user can choose among following objects: dog, cat, fish, smiley, a flower or a tree. The widget also works in the background as a wallpaper so that user can see it even if he or she is not using the application. The widget contains a motivational figure, the last value of diabetes, calories burned that day, a maximum number of points, status of points and the current level where the user is currently located. Based on the changes in figures (it gets smaller when there is no activity and it gets bigger when the activity is performed) the user gets the feedback on physical activities made and on progress in them. The purpose of the figure is initially to allow user to see a feedback on his work and also to encourage and motivate him to be more active once the figure is smaller.

5.3 WIDGET: USE INSTRUCTIONS

Since the main objective of the widget is to motivate the individual to be more active, I wanted to make a widget that changes only with user´s contribution to its changes. This means that a widget is supposed to work on the basis of levels achieved by the user. The more active the user, the higher level accomplished.

In total there are 10 levels that the user can achieve by performing the physical ativity. Each level has 10 points that the user gets as a reward for achieved level. With each level, the selected figure grows. User can reach daily a maximum of 10 points. Each day the user loses 10% of points he/she has achieved in that day. The main goals are to motivate the user to grow faster the figure at the lower levels and to make it difficult at the higher levels to achieve the maximum. The reached maximal levels will recede if the user does not continue with physical activity. The goal is to keep figure big. Points are given based on calories burned per day (1 point is 50 burned calories).

The DiaSport application aims to make the life for an older diabetic easier by encouraging the motivation for physical activity and therby aiding in the treatment of diabetes. Entire management is supposed to be done in an interesting, fun and challenging way.

CHAPTER 6 EVALUATING DIASPORT IN A DEPLOYMENT STUDY

This chapter brings forward results from the testing and evaluation phase. It starts with bringing forward results from the log data analysis followed by survey data analysis. Finally, an overview of study research questions and their solutions are presented.

Analyzing the log data brought interesting results.

Application usage

8 study participants used the DiaSport application each day for 2-weeks study even though they used the application in an additional mobile phone. Of the remaining two participants, participant P10   used the application for only first 6 days while second participant (P8) had only one day without using the application. The frequency of using the application each day for each study participant is presented in the Appendix. Below presented figure 14, is demonstration of one participant´s usage frequency.

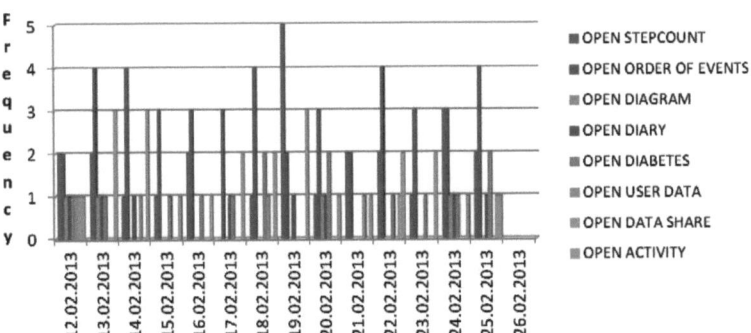

Figure 14 The frequency of using the application throughout the 2 weeks-study; participant P2

Through the above presented diagram of frequency usage and frequency usage of other participants (see Appendix) it is evident that 8 participants had used the application every day. Results have also shown that the application had been used more than once per day what proves that participants had integrated the DiaSport into their everyday life during these 2 weeks. The following diagram demonstrates these results.

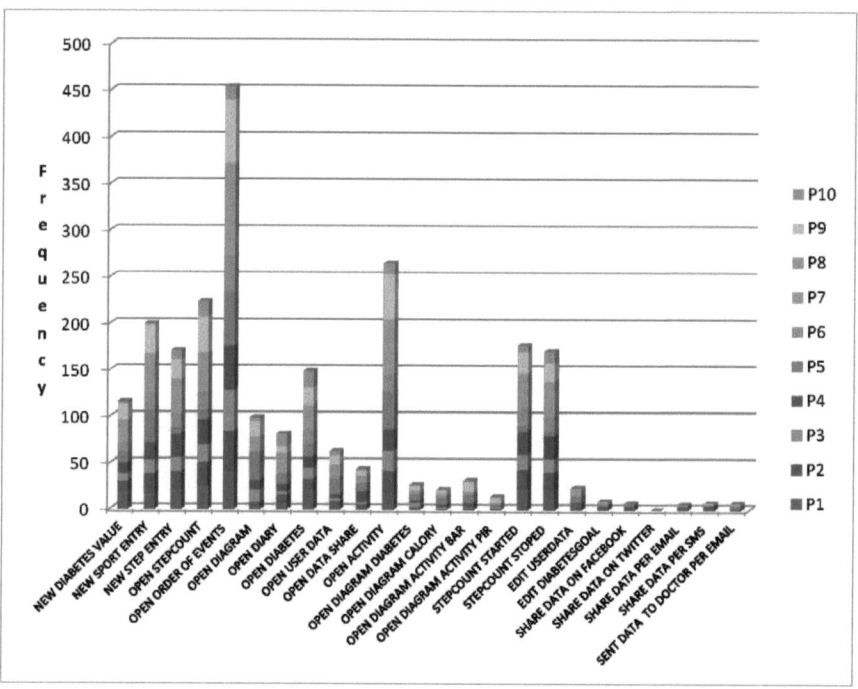

Figure 15 Overall usage frequency of the application

It is obvious that the most used activities are; overview of diabetes and physical activities followed by new activity and step count. An additional evidence that they used application daily for physical activity management are their achieved "game" levels (5 participants achieved maximal 10th level, 3 of them 9th, 1 8th and 1 participant achieved 1st level- the one that used the application for only 6 days).

Information share

As already mentioned, one of aims of the qualitative research was to explore how sharing diabetes information might influence the motivation and in which way it could facilitate the everyday life of an individual. Qualitative data results revealed that sharing information is not important for participants. The data from the above presented diagram confirms the results from the qualitative research. There was a either minimal or even no use of share activities (especially twitter). For a better overview of the data, figure 16 shows clear results.

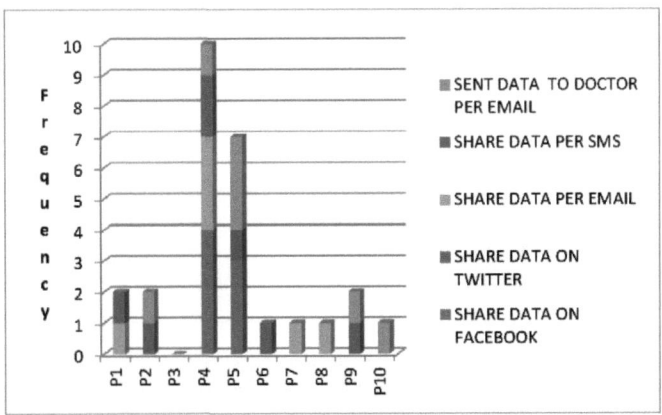

Figure 16 Overall usage frequency of share data activities

The most commonly used share activities are: share per sms and email to share information with the doctor. It is clear that the activity "twitter" is not used at all. Facebook usage was also minimal, which is not surprising for elderly since they are not as familiar with social networks as younger people are. Since there is no activity that was used consistently throughout the testing period, the assumption from the beginning of the research, that social media might have potential in the self-management is unjustified. Since 2-weeks are a short time to make any final claims, I will not argue that share activities have no potential in mobile application self-management concept. Participants who mostly used share activities are the youngest study participants (P5=51 and P4=53). The results on the individual use of share activities are provided in the appendix.

Self-management using DiaSport application

How did the application contribute to participants with regards to the self-management, can be seen through the following diagram.

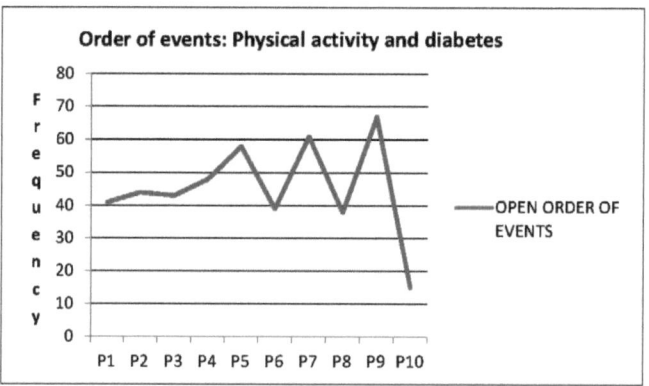

Figure 17 The overall frequency of chosen activity „order of events (physical activity and diabetes)"

The only participant, P10 , who used the application for the first 6 days, contributed to the fall of the line. Other users, used the overview of their performed activities and entered diabetes values up to 70 times during the 2- week study.

Usage of physical activity management

Since the main focus of this work is diabetes self- management through management of physical activities, the following diagrams demonstrate the usage frequency for each participant for two physical activity options: new sport entry and new step entry.

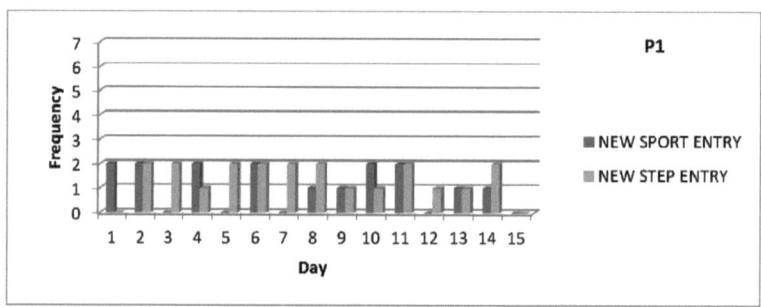

Figure 18 The frequency of activities new sport- and new step entry; participant P1

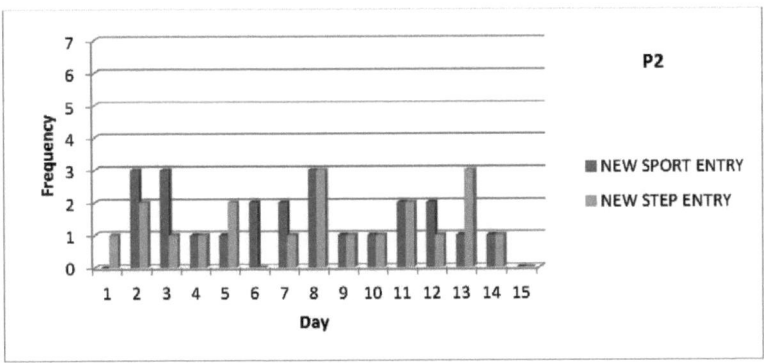

Figure 19 The frequency of activities new sport- and new step entry; participant P2

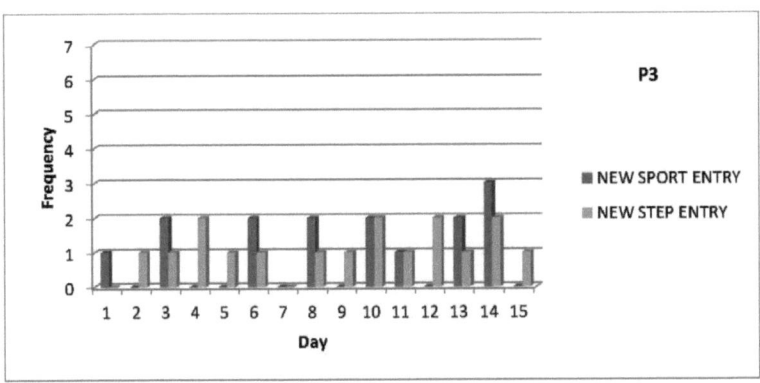

Figure 20 The frequency of activities new sport- and new step entry; participant P3

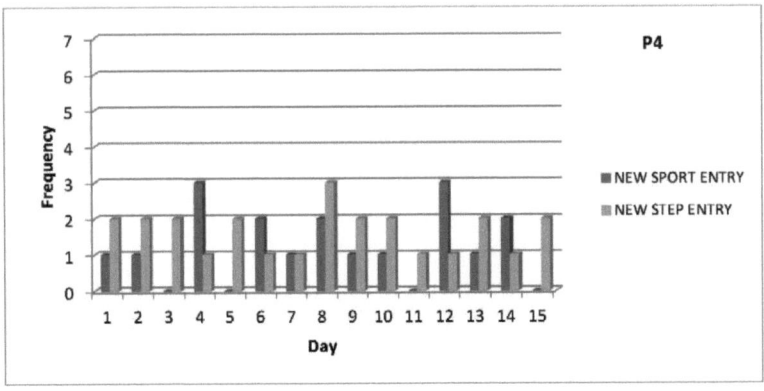

Figure 21 The frequency of activities new sport- and new step entry; participant P4

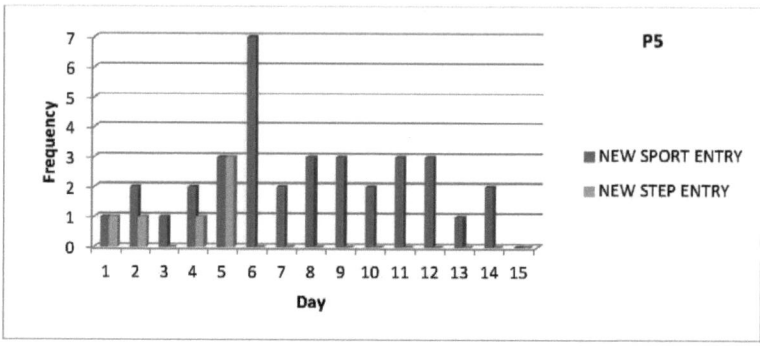

Figure 22 The frequency of activities new sport- and new step entry; participant P5

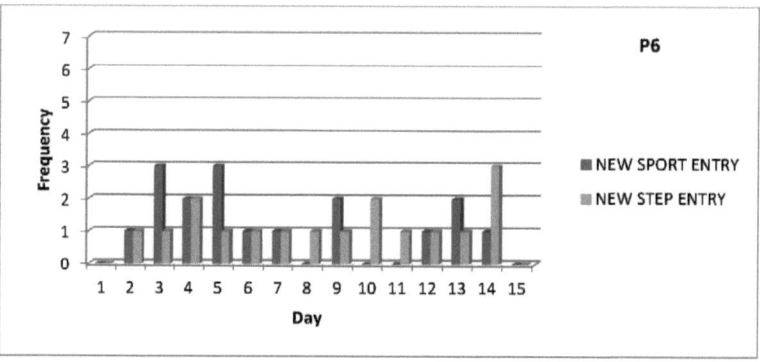

Figure 23 The frequency of activities new sport- and new step entry; participant P6

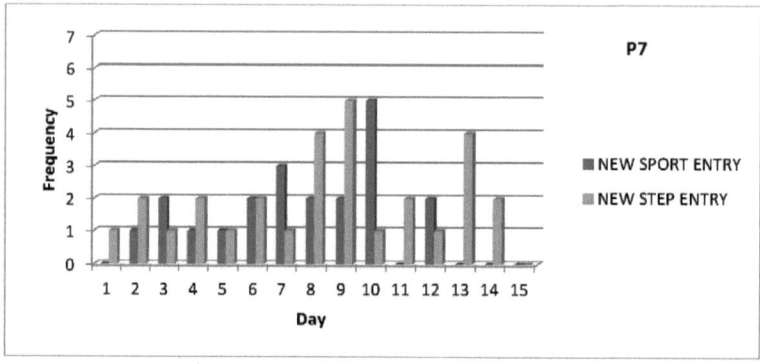

Figure 24 The frequency of activities new sport- and new step entry; participant P7

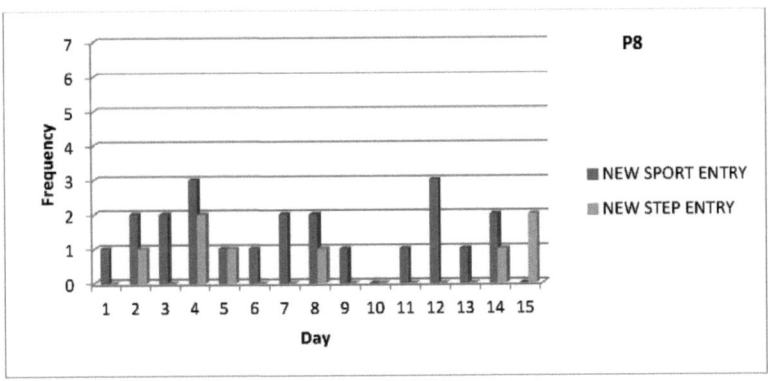

Figure 25 the frequency of activities new sport- and new step entry; participant P8

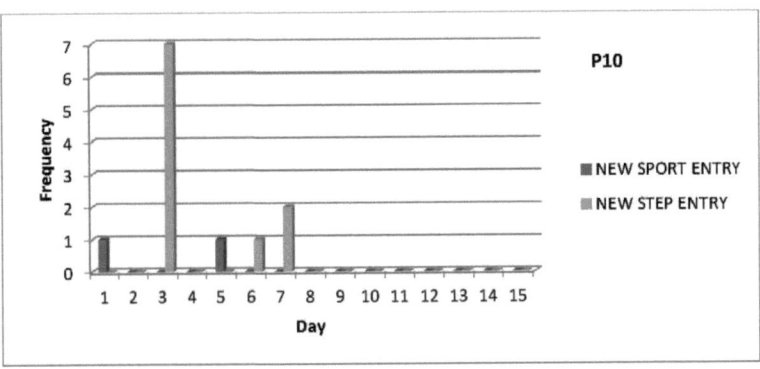

Figure 26 The frequency of activities new sport- and new step entry; participant P10

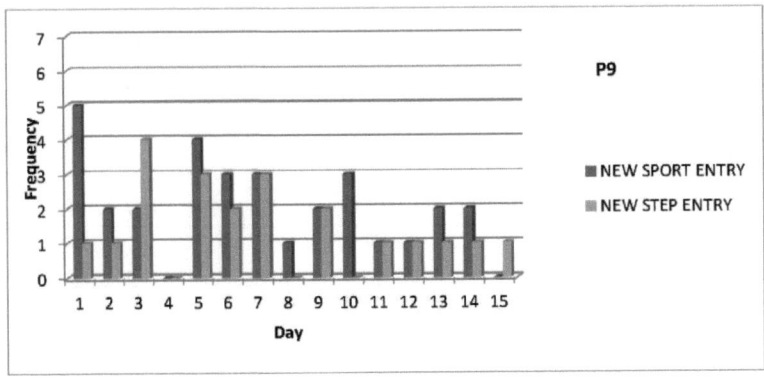

Figure 27 The frequency of activities new sport- and new step entry; participant P9

It is clear to see that almost every participant used these activities every day. This leads to conclusion that the most used activities are exactly those that were from greatest importance for this study.

To summarize results for all participants, diagram below is presented.

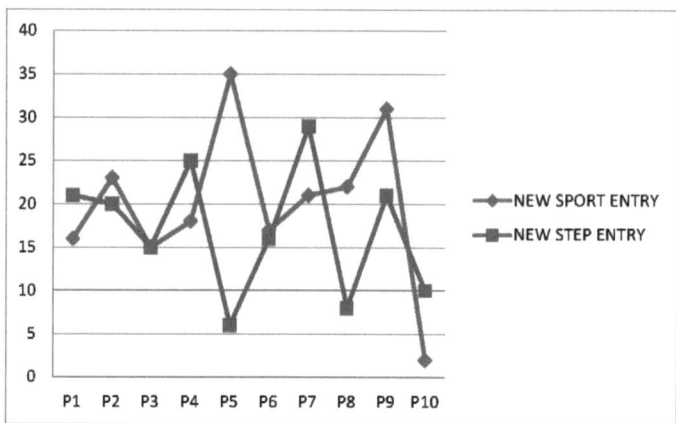

Figure 28 The frequency of activities new sport- and new step entry; all participants

Findings from the quantitative data analysis have revealed following results.

Overall impression

9 participants have rated the DiaSport as a very good application. The scores were given on a 5-point Likert scale from 1 to 5 , where 1 equals very good and 5 equals not good at all. Following table represents clear results.

How well do you find the DiSport application in total? Please give your opinion on a school grading scale of 1 to 5, where 1 = very good to 5 = not good at all

		Frequency	Percent	Valid Percent	Cumulative Percent
Valid	very good	9	90,0	100,0	100,0
Missing	don´t know	1	10,0		
Total		10	100,0		

Table 7 Descriptive statistic; overall DiaSport impression

Since the participant P10   did not use the application long enough to make any ratings, she did not participate in the evaluation phase.

Usability

Even though usability has been tested through the log data analysis, I found the same results through testing quantitative survey data.

How often have you used DiaSport application?

		Frequency	Percent	Valid Percent	Cumulative Percent
Valid	several times per week	1	10,0	11,1	11,1
	everyday	3	30,0	33,3	44,4
	several times per day	5	50,0	55,6	100,0
	Total	9	90,0	100,0	
Missing	System	1	10,0		
Total		10	100,0		

Table 8 DiaSport usability

The mode of 5 confirms the results from log data analysis, where results revealed that the majority of participants used the application several times per day.

How often have you used DiaSport?

N	Valid	9
	Missing	1
Mean		4,4444
Mode		5,00

Table 9 DiaSport usability mean value

Self-management concept efficiency

The following diagram presents the perceived self-management efficiency.

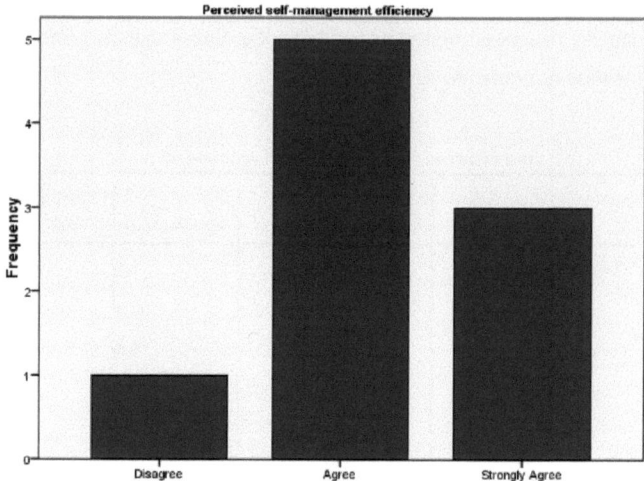

Figure 29 Self-management efficiency, descriptive statistics

The mean value of 4 indicates that participants were rather satisfied with the DiaSport as a diabetes-self-management tool.

Motivational figures

I find these motivation figures really interesting.

		Frequency	Percent	Valid Percent	Cumulative Percent
Valid	Neutral	1	10,0	11,1	11,1
	Agree	1	10,0	11,1	22,2
	Strongly Agree	7	70,0	77,8	100,0
	Total	9	90,0	100,0	
Missing	System	1	10,0		
Total		10	100,0		

Figure 30 Descriptive statistics, motivational figures

From the figure above it is apparent that 8 out of 9 participants who were testing the application for whole 2-weeks found motivational figures interesting and motivating.

Functionality

Functions are easy to learn.

		Frequency	Percent	Valid Percent	Cumulative Percent
Valid	Neutral	2	20,0	22,2	22,2
	Agree	5	50,0	55,6	77,8
	Strongly Agree	2	20,0	22,2	100,0
	Total	9	90,0	100,0	
Missing	System	1	10,0		
Total		10	100,0		

Table 10 Descriptive statistics; functionality

7 participants found DiaSport functions easy to learn and 2 participants were undecided.

Future usage intention

I will continue using the app.

		Frequency	Percent	Valid Percent	Cumulative Percent
Valid	probably not	2	20,0	22,2	22,2
	probably	3	30,0	33,3	55,6
	pretty probably	3	30,0	33,3	88,9
	definitely	1	10,0	11,1	100,0
	Total	9	90,0	100,0	
Missing	System	1	10,0		
Total		10	100,0		

Table 11 Descriptive statistics; future usage intention

Since 8 persons have an intention of using the DiaSport application in the future, I can conclude that it has a potential of facilitating diabetes self-management concept.

Answers to open ended questions are presented in the table below.

What do you like about the application?	What would you like to change?
I like the design. Motivational figures are great and entire concept is phenomenal.	I would like to add the calorie-table.
The step counter is simply perfect.	Diagrams should be bigger.
I loved figures the most. It made my days fun.	Bread values should be integrated.
I loved the simplicity. It is really easy to use it. I found everything pretty fast.	Motivational figures are too feminine. There should be an option of sharing the widget with others, rather then sharing other information.
I liked the entire idea; it made me feel responsible for it and therefore made me be active just to see how flowers grow.	Diagrams are small. If you stop or pause the step counter, nothing changes and you never know if you have clicked it or not.

Table 12 Answers to open ended survey questions

Results show that participants liked the application even though they had used it only for 2 weeks. Motivational figures seem to be very appreciated by participants. The simplicity and easy using of the application has made it be accepted by study participants. Some propositions for changes are; integration of the calorie table, bread values and smaller diagrams.

CHAPTER 7 DISCUSSION AND FUTURE WORK

In this paper, I have presented the mobile application DiaSport that has the potential to serve to older people diagnosed with Type 2 diabetes as a self-management tool. Application is used in Android phones and contains, besides the integrated step counter, additional features that encourage diabetics to be physically active. This type of application can assist elderly diabetics in their physical activity self-management by providing them an all-in-one service; surveillance of physical activities, calorie consumption and diabetes value. The user is additionally provided with a personal diary where he/she can take notes and with an overview of all actions performed within one day. With the widget that is primarily designed to encourage the motivation, diabetic is able to manage everyday activities in an interesting and fun way. Through qualitative and quantitative data collected from participants who tested and evaluated the application, I found that the overall satisfaction of the participants regarding the application was positive. Almost all participants used the application several times per day. Results revealed that the most used activities were those associated with the physical activity. Most participants found step counter and motivational figures to be very useful and interesting. Results also showed that participants are interested in using the application in the future. Since for the application testing phase participants were provided with Android telephones, all were interested in whether they can install the application on their phone. Interest for future use is therefore obvious.

However, there are few limitations of the study. Effectiveness and usefulness of the application are non- trivial. Since this was a 2-week study it is not to completely rely on the findings. Due to the short testing period, I was not able to make any claims about how did the application fit into everyday life of participants in the long run. It is possible that participants were using the application because they knew they are participating in the study and that without their cooperation this study would not be possible. It is questionable how they would use the application in the long run.

Additional critical point of view is that the participants were not interviewed after the testing phase to examine their attitudes about the functionality, efficiency and usability. It is therefore to rely on the quantitative data obtained from the survey. The data revealed that majority of participants evaluated positively the functionality, design, efficiency and usability. Yet, doing a final qualitative interview might have offered additional / complementary insight and give the opportunity to explore some of their experiences in more detail than accomplished with a survey. The reason why the final qualitative interview was not conducted is that I assumed that the information obtained through the survey and 3 open-ended questions regarding their opinion on the application were sufficient. Even though the qualitative survey data is valuable and have opened the door for further work on the application, the data from qualitative in-depth interviews would be more elaborately.

Since the majority of participants were recruited through the sport union, data about how application motivates older people are controversial. Since these people already have the physical activity involved in their life, it is questionable how would the application encourage the person who was not performing any physical activity during the week. Since this was a small sample study it is not possible to generalize results either for people who perform some type of physical activity or for others, who do not perform any activity.

As already stated in the findings, the application has several disadvantages: small diagrams, feminine motivational figures and the lack of possibility to share the widget image through social media. The last disadvantage indicates that even though results showed that participants were sceptic about sharing their diabetes information, they might be willing to share it through an interesting way such as through sharing the widget image. This leads to a conclusion that sharing the personal information might not be an option, but sharing the personal achievement such as that achieved through growing the widget image might be from a great importance for older diabetics. The work of Grosinger et al., (2012) suggests that involving older adults with their close friends and encouraging together the physical activity might be helpful. Therefore the AgileLife was made. The source of potential error in my study could be the inadequacy of properly presenting the information share option. This confirms the potential importance of sharing achievement with others as stated in many studies like Lin et al. (2006) and Grosinger et al. (2012). Yet, it is difficult to assess the potential importance of the information share options since this study was conducted with Austrian participants whose culture is known as an individualistic culture explained earlier in this work. Results from this study also confirm the importance of creative motivational figures such as those presented in DiaSport, UbiFit and Fish´n´Steps applications.

In order to properly detect impact of the DiaSport on elderly diabetics it might be necessary to conduct the study with more participants (in hundreds or thousands) over a longer period of time (several months). It would also be necessary to make small modifications on the application, such as larger diagrams, figures modified to satisfy both sexes and interesting way to share information, for example, sharing the widget image. It would be essential to include participants in the evaluation phase through in-depth interviews in order to get an better understanding of how did the aplication fit and changed their lives. It would be an interesting future work to offer a training and nutritional plan for an individual and an option of involving friends (chat) into the discussion about that plan. An additional proposition for the future work would be a mobile application for obese adults that are not diseased with Type II diabetes.

In order to summarize entire set of research questions covered in this study and solutions to those, the following table is presented.

RESEARCH QUESTION	SOLUTIONS
1. How do elderly diabetics perceive the disease and what is their understanding of correlation between the disease and the lifestyle (physical activity)?	Elderly diabetics are aware of the physical activity importance for facilitating Type II diabetes.
2. What motivates elderly diabetics to be physically active?	Usually, they are motivated if they experience bad diabetes value and gained weight. They are also motivated if they see results after they perform activities.
3. How important is the social support in motivating elderly diabetics to be physically active?	Social support from immediate family is only important.
3.1 Are diabetics comfortable with sharing information regarding their activity level?	Elderly diabetics are not comfortable with sharing information.

4. How elderly diabetics perceive the need for diabetes self-management?	Elderly diabetics find self-management concept as very useful and as a necessity in facilitating the disease.
5. How effective is the mobile application as the diabetes self-management tool that an elderly diabetic can smoothly integrate into his/her everyday life while effectively encouraging physical activity?	DiaSport has a great potential as the self-management tool.
5.1 Which way should be used to design constant reminder/feedback about activity goals?	Aesthetic figure should be used as a reminder of low activity level. This should be used as wallpaper in the background.
5.2 What is the best way to present an emotional state based on daily goals?	Growing figure if activity increased and vice a verse.

Table 13 An overview of research questions and solutions

CHAPTER 8 CONCLUSION

In summary, the findings from the study of the DiaSport application have shown that encouraging elderly diabetics with a mobile application to be more physically active is promising. Furthermore the smartphone as a platform was mostly well received and easy to interact with. By spending lots of time with elderly diabetics I have learnt that the supportive technology holds a great potential in the treatment of the Type II diabetes and the importance of considering individual needs of diabetics once designing the application that is a potential self-management tool. Therefore, DiaSport application was designed to fulfill desires and needs of an elderly group of people by providing them with simplicity, functionality and effectiveness at the same time.

BIBLIOGRAPHY

Aarhus R., Ballegaard A.S., Hansen R. T. (2009). The eDiary: Bridging home and hospital through healthcare technology. In Proceedings of ECSCW 2009, 63-84.

Ainsworth, B.E. (2000). Compendium of Physical Activities: an update of activity codes and MET intensities. In: Medicine & Science in Sports & Exercise. International Life Sciences Institute, p498-p516.

American Diabetes Association. (2003). Physical Activity/Exercise and Diabetes Mellitus. Diabetes care, volume 26, supplement 1 p73-p77.

Antipatis V.J. and Gill T.P. (2001). Epidemiology: Obesity as a Global Problem.Rowett Research Institute. Aberdeen, UK

Årsand E., TataraN., Østengen G., Hartvigsen G. (2010). Mobile Phone-Based Self-Management Tools for Type 2 Diabetes: The Few Touch Application. Journal of Diabetes Science and Technology p328–336.

Bieber G., Koldrack P., Sablowski C., Peter C., Urban B. (2010). Mobile physical actiity recognition of Stand-Up and Sit-Down Transitions for User Behaviour Analysis. PETRA '10 Proceedings of the 3rd International Conference on Pervasive Technologies Related to Assistive Environments.

Bielik P., Tomlein M., Kratky P., Mitrik S., Barla M., Bielikova M. (2012). Move2Play: An Innovative Approach to Encouraging People to Be More Physically Active. IHI '12

Birnbauer/Frauenschuh. (2008). Besser Bewegen. St. Pölten: zitiert in: NÖGUS – Agentur für Gesundheitsvorsorge (Hg.)

Blake, H. (2008). Innovation in practice: mobile phone technology in patient care. Nottingham: British Journal of Community Nursing Volume 13, number 4

Boule N.G., Haddad E., Kenny G.P., Wells G.A., Sigal R.J. (2001). Effects of Excercise on Glycemic Control and Body Massin Type 2 Diabetes Mellitus; A Meta-aalysis of Controlled Clinical Trials. Ottawa: JAMA, Volume 286, number 10, p1218-1227.

Bravata D.M., Smith-Spangler C., Sundaram V., Gienger A.L., Lewis R., Stave C.D., Olkin I., Sirad J.R. (2007). Using Pedometers to Increase Physical Activity and Improve Health: A Systematic Review. JAMA, 298(19), p2296-2304.

Byrne R., Eslambolchilar P. (2010). Encouraging an Active Lifestyle with Personal Mobile. MobileHCI 2010

CDC. (2011). Centers for Disease Control and Prevention Retrieved February 15, 2013 http://www.cdc.gov/chronicdisease/resources/publications/aag/obesity.htm

Chomutare T., Fernandez-Luque L., Årsand E., Hartvigsen G. (2011). Features of Mobile Diabetes Applications: Review of the Literature and Analysis of Current Applications Compared Against Evidence-Based Guidelines. Journal of Medical Internet Research, Volume 13

Chopra M., Galbraith S., Darnton-Hill I. (2002). A global response to a global problem: the epidemic. Special Theme – Global Public Health and International Law, Bulletin of the World Health Organization 2002

Consolvo S., Everitt K., SmithI., Landey A.J. (2006). Design Requirements for Technologies that Encourage Physical Activity. CHI 2006 Proceedings, Designing for Tangible Interactions. p. 457-466

Consolvo S., McDonald W.D., Toscos T., Chen M.Y., Froehlich J., Harrison B., Klasnja P., LaMarca A., LeGrand L., Libby R., Smith I., Landay A.J. (2008). Activity Sensing in the Wild: A field Trial of UbiFit Garden.CHI 2008 Proceedings, Personal Health p.1797-1806

Corbin C.B., Welk G.J., Lindsey R. (2000). Using Self-Management Skills to Adhere to Healthy Lifestyle Behaviors. In Concepts of Physical Fitness: Active Lifestyles for Wellness 10th edition. Mcgraw-Hill Higher edition: 2000:71-4.

Davies M.J., Heller S., Skinner T.C., Campbell M.J., Carey M.E., Cradock S., Dallosso H.M., Daly H., Doherty Y., Eaton S., Fox C., Oliver L., Rantell K., Rayman G., Khunti K. (2007). Effectiveness of the diabetes education and self management for ongoing and newly diagnosed (DESMOND) programme for people with newly diagnosed Type 2 diabetes: cluster randomised controlled trial. British Medical Journal (BMJ), p1-11.

Diabetes.co.uk the global diabetes community. (n.d.). Retrieved february 20, 2013 http://www.diabetes.co.uk/what-is-hba1c.html

Glaser, B. G. (2002). Conceptualization: On Theory and Theorizing Using Grounded Theory. International Journal of Qualitative Methods 1 (2) Spring 2002.

Grosinger J., Vetere F., Fitzpatrick G. (2012) Agile Life: Addressing Knowledge and Social Motivations for Active Aging, OZCHI'12

Helmrich S., Ragland D.R., Leung R.W., Paffenbarger R.S. (1991). Physical activity and reduced occurence of non-insulin-dependent diabetes mellitus. The New England Journal Of Medicine, Volume 325, number 3, p147- p152.

Heyward, V. (2013). Human Kinetics: The Information Leader in Physical Activity and Health. Retrieved February 17, 2013 http://www.humankinetics.com/excerpts/excerpts/using-technology-to-promote-physical-activity

Hofstede (n.d.) Individualism / Collectivism. Retrieved March 13, 2013 http://www.andrews.edu/~tidwell/bsad560/HofstedeIndividualism.html

Horita Y., Sekine M., Tamura T. Yutaka K., Yuji H., Toshiro F. (2008). New attempt of proposing the pedometer algorithm in the elderly. Medical Devices and Biosensors, 2008, 5th International Summer School and Symposium p. 111 - 112

Hu F.B., Manson J.E., Stampfer M.J., Colditz G., Liu S., Solomon C.G., Willet W.C. (2001). Diet,lifestyle and the risk of Type 2 diabetes mellitus in women. N Engl J Med, Volume 345, number 11 p. 790-797.

Hurling R., Catt M., De Boni M., Fairley B.W., Hurst T., Murray P., MPhil C., Richardson A., Sodhi J.S. (2007). Using internet and Mobile Phone Technology to Deliver an Automated Physical Activity Program: Randomized Controlled Trial. Journal of Medical Internet Research, Volume 9, Issue 2

Khan, A. M. (2011). Human Activity Recognition Using A Single Tri-axial. Seoul, Department of Computer Engineering, Graduate School,Kyung Hee University, Korea.

Klasnja P, Consolvo S., McDonald W. D., Landay A.J., Prett W. (2009). Using Mobile and Personal Sensing Technologies to Support Health Behaviour Change in Everyday Life:Lessons Learned. AMIA 2009 p338-342.

Lin J.J,Mamykina L., Lindtne S.,Dalajoux G., Strub H.B. (2006). Fish´n´Steps: Encouraging Physical Activity with an Interactive Computer Game. P.Dourish and A.Friday (Eds.): Ubicomp 2006, LNCS 4206, p 261-278

Lin J.J., Mamkyina L., Lindtner S., Delajoux G. and Strub H.B. (2006). Fish´n´Steps: Encouraging Physical Activity with an Interactive Computer Game. Springer-Verlag Berlin Heidelberg, p261-278 .

Mamykina L. (2009). Supporting Diabetes Management Practices with Ubiquitous Computing. CHI 2009

Mamykina L., Miller A.D., Mynatt E.D.and Greenblatt D. (2010). Constructing Identities through Storytelling in Diabetes Management. CHI 2010

Mamykina L., Mynatt D.E., Davidson P.R, Greenblatt D. (2008). MAHI: Investigation of Social Scaffolding for Reflective Thinking in Diabetes Management. CHI 2008

Mamykina L., Mynatt E.D. (2007). Investigating and Supporting Health Management Practices of Individuals with Diabetes. HealthNet 2007, p49-54.

Mamykina L., Mynatt E.D., Kaufman D. (2006). Investigating Health Management Practices of Individuals with Diabetes. CHI 2006

Morley, J. E. (1998). The Elderly Type 2 Diabetic Patient:Special Considerations. Diabetic medicine, Volume 15 Suppl. 4, p41–46.

Morrow, S. and Smith, M. (1995). A grounded theory study: Construction of survival and coping by women who have survived childhood sexual abuse. In John Cresswell (Ed.), Qualitatuve inquiry and research design: Choosing among five traditions (pp.297-321). Thousand Oaks, CA: SAGE.

Orzano, A. J. & Scott, J. G. (2004). Diagnosis and Treatment of Obesity in Adults:. Department of Family Medicine. Somerset, NJ: J Am Board Fam Med.

Österreichische Diabetes Gesellschaft (ÖDG). Diabetes Typ 2: Vermeidbare Volkskrankheit (n.d.) Retrieved February 14, 2013 http://www.oedg.org/diabetes.html

Österreichische Gesundheitsportal (2012). Öffentliches gesundheitsportal Österreichs: Energieverbrauch bei körperlichen Aktivitäten & Sport. Retrieved February 20, 2013, https://www.gesundheit.gv.at/Portal.Node/ghp/public/content/Energieverbrauch_Aktivitaeten.html

Preuveneers D., Berbers Y. (2008). Mobile Phones Assisting With Health Self-Care: a Diabetes Case Study. Proceedings of the 10th international conference on Human computer interaction with mobile devices and services

Siemens Global Website. (n.d.) Retrieved March 10, 2013 http://www.siemens.com/innovation/de/publikationen/zeitschriften_pictures_of_the_future/pof_fruehjahr_2007 /lebenswerte_megacities/home_care_und_telemedizin.htm

Soares, A.M., Farhangmehr, M., Shoham, A. (2007). Hofstede´s Dimension of Culture inInternational Marketing Studies. Journal of Business Research 60(3), pp.227-284.

Tuomilehto J., Lindström J., Eriksson J., Valle T.T., Hämäläinen H.,Ilanne-Parikka P., Keinänen-Kiukaanniemi S., Laakso M., Louheranta A., Rastas M., Salminen V., Uusitupa M. (2001). Prevention of Type 2 diabetes mellitus by changes in lifestyle among subjects with impaired glucose tolerance. N Engl J Med, Volume 344, number 18, p1343-1350.

Valdez A.C., Ziefle M., Horstmann A., Herding D., Schroeder U. (2010). Mobile Devices Used for Medical Applications: Insights Won from a Usability Study with Diabetes Patients. International Journal of Digital Siciety (IJDS),Volume 1, Issue 4

WHO. (1999). Definition, Diagnosis and Classification of Diabetes Mellitus and its Complications. Geneva: World Health Organization, Department of Noncommunicable Disease Surveillance.

WHO. (2012). World Health Organization: Diabetes:Key facts Retrieved February 14, 2013 http://www.who.int/mediacentre/factsheets/fs312/en/index.html

WHO. (2012). World Health Organization: Obesity and overweight Retrieved February 15, 2013 http://www.who.int/mediacentre/factsheets/fs311/en/

Wisegeek. What Is Social Desirability Bias? (n.d.) Retrieved February 23, 2013, http://www.wisegeek.com/what-is-social-desirability-bias.htm

Zeyfang A., Braun A., Wernecke J. (2011). Mitteilungen der Deutsche Diabetes-Stiftung (DDS); Diabetes Mellitus im Alter Teil 2. Der Diabetologe 2011 7: p139-142.

Zhu, W. (2008). Promoting Physical Activity Using Technology. President´s Council on Physical Fitness and Sports; Research Digest Series 9, number 3, p1-8.

Printed by Books on Demand GmbH, Norderstedt / Germany